Praise for

TEN TREASURES
STRATEGIC PLAYBOOK

"Mark Daly shares his secrets from years of successfully founding businesses and from strategically building other businesses. Mark is a great friend. He is also a brilliant strategist. *Ten Treasures* will help businesses be more profitable, and of special interest to me, achieve a healthier culture. Take a journey as told through Joseph and Elizabeth as they experience Mark's strategic playbook."
—Dave Dillon, 3M, Hallmark, Union Pacific boards,
Former CEO, Kroger

"Mark has been a long-time strategic confidant and mentor to me and our business over decades. *Ten Treasures* is truly the 'best of' Mark, and his strategic frameworks that have been time-tested and successful for many great companies. The book is a straightforward, practical guide to differentiating your company, both inside and out, to create a winning strategy in your market. Mark developed a playbook for senior managers, while wrapping it in a great story with incredible people, to help the audience really experience each treasure. A must read for entrepreneurs, business owners, and leaders!"
—Lisa Jennings, President & CEO,
PMC SMART Solutions

"One of the best business books I've ever read! All the major content of a graduate business course, but presented in an easy to read story. This is a must-read for any new manager or for an experienced manager who is looking to take their management experience to the next level."
—Kevin Bright, Managing Director,
Duke Energy

"I absolutely love this book! I look forward to seeing it as the bestselling business book on the NYT's best seller list. Thanks for bringing it to life. I found it easy to read, compelling, practical, and comprehensive. I am buying copies to hand out to all the leaders in our company with the first one going to my daughter (Katherine) as her strategic playbook for leading the company in the future."
—Steve Steinman, Chairman & CEO,
Sims-Lohman (Inc 5000)

"This is fantastic! Very original approach...the tone and passion are consistent throughout...inspired me to implement many of the concepts."
—Alan Abram, CFO, Sur-Seal Corporation

"Love it! I'm going to follow it!"
—Lisa Pruett, Chief Sales & Marketing Officer, Downlite

"The intriguing Ten Treasures framework drew me in. I like the diversity of the sages, especially the lesser known ones, and how each of their stories links to a clearly laid out strategy in the playbook. Anyone interested in growing as a leader or sustaining a successful business will get insights and practical ideas they can put to use right away."
—Joanne Spigner, Founding Partner, VisionFirst

"I have known Mark Daly for 22 years. He has been one of my top business advisors during that time. I've known Mark to be an exemplary strategist, a world class musician, a remarkable artist, and a great friend. After reading the Ten Treasures, I can now tie all of his 'off the chart' virtues into a single collection of anecdotes. I know firsthand, the dream journeys were authentic and impactful because I have observed many of these leadership themes and professional management tools from my own experiences."
—Steve Cobb, Chairman, Henny Penny Corporation

The

TEN

Map

TREASURES

to Enduring

STRATEGIC

Business Success

PLAYBOOK

Mark Daly

Publisher:
DSA (Daly Strategic Associates, Inc.) Cincinnati, Ohio
Web Sites: DalyStrategic.com, TenTreasures.com

Library of Congress Cataloging-in-Publication Data:
Daly, Mark, 1956—author.
Ten Treasures Strategic Playbook / Mark Daly.
        p. cm.

First Edition. Includes bibliographical references and index.

Identifiers:
ISBN 978-1-7338327-2-4 (hardcover)
ISBN 978-1-7338327-1-7 (paperback)
ISBN 978-1-7338327-0-0 (eBook)
Library of Congress Control Number: 2019902940

Subjects: 1. Success in business. 2. Leadership. 3. Strategic planning. 4. Business planning.
I. Title. II. Title: Ten Treasures.   Title: 10 Treasures.   Title: Strategic Playbook.

Editor, Gregg Daly

Cover Concept: Art Direction: Jeff Walker, Design: Ian O'Saben, VSA Partners, Inc.

Other Books by Mark Daly:

5 Steps To Board Success! New Approaches to Board Effectiveness and Business Success / Mark Daly/ AuthorHouse, 2005

Printed in the United States of America

DSA

To
Gigi, my
wonderful wife
I am truly blessed and
lucky to share life with you
And to Gregg, Steven, and Patrick
Love
All ways
and Always

CONTENTS

Foreword   viii

Introduction   x

Prologue: Seeking Treasure   1
   How Do You Win Monopoly?   3
   A Playbook with a CURVE   12
   Midnight Dreams   20

1   Define The Dream (Treasure 1)   21
   Defining a Dream with FATE   23
   A TRUE Goal   31
   Strategic Dashboard   36
   Beautiful Dreams   38

2   Niche The New (Treasure 2)   43
   Gravity-Shifts, Niches & Riches   44
   The Master Spotter (Innovator)   46
   Absolute Advantage   55
   3-Keys-Strategy   56
   One More Thing   63

3   Tap The Top Talent (Treasure 3)   68
   Preparing to Succeed   70
   Five Steps To Top Talent   73
   Identify and Nurture Stars   82
   Five Steps To Successful Succession   84

4   Operational Discipline: Helps You Win (Treasure 4)   94
   Ford's Recipe for Success   96
   Lean Forward With Lean Techniques   103
   Value Chain Breakthroughs   106
   As The Wheel Turns   113

5   Elevate The Elephants (Treasure 5)   118
   Elephants Rule (80/20)   119
   Customers Are Not Equal   126
   Questionable Priorities   133
   Yes, No, & Gray Zones   136
   Elephant Traction   139

6   Pace The Growth (Treasure 6)   143
Faced Paced Dreams   143
Speed Shifts   147
Slinky-Effect   148
Taking Care of Time   150

7   A Unique Position: A Better Decision (Treasure 7)   156
Seeing is Believing   156
Changing Perceptions   160
The Real Battleground   166
Position is Better Than Proposition   166

8   Cultivate A Healthy Culture (Treasure 8)   171
Giving Voice to Values   172
Defining Culture   175
TEAMS^2 Guidelines   181
Values in Action   188
The Platinum Standard   192

9   Make Work Simple (Treasure 9)   196
Simple Sparks & Benchmarks   197
Bash Away Barriers   203
Simple Questions   211
Connected Treasure   214

10 Intentionally Improve (Treasure 10)   220
Paris, Plutonium, and Process Improvement   221
Timeless Improvement Tools   223
Twice Nobel   238

Epilogue: True Treasure   243

Bibliography   244

Image Credits   250

Index   251

Acknowledgements   257

About The Author   259

FOREWORD

Peter Philippi
Strategex Chairman and Founder

Some books become bestsellers because they're engaging and entertaining, an easy and enjoyable read, good while they last and then they sit on a bookshelf gathering dust. Other books become timeless classics, read generation after generation. They become true "literature," must-reads to obtain a well-rounded education.

Mark Daly has written an engaging masterpiece of literature for business success. His endless business contributions to top performing companies make this playbook a must-apply manual for business leaders. A startup will have the benefit of getting on the right path to unimaginable prosperity; a well-established multi-billion-dollar enterprise will enjoy decades of sustainable growth and profitability by making this playbook a strategic part of its DNA.

Mark brings to life ten fascinating historical personalities and ties lessons for business success to them in genius fashion.

I met Mark through his first book. I had come to the place where it became increasingly clear that Strategex needed an outside Board. I embarked on a two-year investigation, talking to every privately held company CEO I could. One business owner emphatically recommended I get ahold of Mark's *5 Steps to Board Success*. After devouring the book and meeting Mark, I asked him to join our Board. What an asset he has proven to be. He's highly respected by the other five Board Members as he contributes with keen insights and strategic direction, unendingly.

His new book, *Ten Treasures Strategic Playbook,* is a manual for business success, a constant companion for business leaders. Struggling with focus? Go to the Elephants Treasure. Challenged on growth? Study the Pace The Growth Treasure. Unclear on how to innovate for future position? Get directions from the Niche The New Treasure. Feeling like you're pushing a rope on improving company culture? Apply the Cultivate a Healthy Culture Treasure.

Keep digging. This Treasure hunt will be thrilling for you. Treat it with the respect it so aptly deserves. Listen to it carefully. Apply it diligently. Share it generously.

INTRODUCTION

Ten Treasures Strategic Playbook began with this simple question: "What would be most useful to you in a new business book?"

Myriad answers from around the world, plus research and insights from my forty years of business experience, reveal what people want and need in a new business book.

Ten Treasures, Ten Chapters, Ten Successes

Ten Treasures focuses on ten important areas for improvement where businesses and organizations underperform. It provides you with an indispensable map or *strategic playbook* to solve and prevent these costly problems from occurring in the future. It guides you through ten proven, integrated leadership paths to enduring success.

The improvement areas are covered in ten chapters called treasures. You experience and learn the main lesson of each treasure through intimate visits with wise sages at crucial moments in their lives. The treasures provide you with:

1. **A More Vivid Future With More Potential**— Leadership tools that define a clearer future to realize greater success beyond just profit (Treasure 1, Define The Dream, Dr. Martin Luther King Jr).

2. **Improved Innovation Abilities**—Strategy techniques that transform ideas and innovation into unique competitive advantages (Treasure 2, Niche The New, Steve Jobs).

3. **The Right Talent**—Proven processes to recruit, retain, and sustain the right top talent (Treasure 3, Tap The Top Talent, Coach John Wooden).

4. **Lower Costs, More Competitive Operations**—Breakthrough methods that reduce costs and advance operational excellence and competitive advantage (Treasure 4, Operational Discipline: Helps You Win, Henry Ford).

5. **Better Priorities, More Time**—More time to do the important. Priorities will improve using 80/20 paradigms that use fewer resources to realize more victories (Treasure 5, Elevate The Elephants, Vilfredo Pareto).

6. **A Faster Pace With Less Waste**—Powerful ways to manage and accelerate the pace of growth and effectively move projects forward in less time (Treasure 6, Pace The Growth, Genghis Khan).

7. **More Profitable Positioning**—Unique positioning concepts that build on customer insights and truths to sell and earn more (Treasure 7, A Unique Position: A Better Decision, Giotto di Bondone).

8. **A Healthier Culture**—Leadership principles to create a purposeful and distinct culture with more meaningful and actionable values (Treasure 8, Cultivate A Healthy Culture, Eleanor Roosevelt).

9. **Simplified Work**—Approaches that make work easier to do by removing unhealthy barriers, complexity, and frustration (Treasure 9, Make Work Simple, Alexander Calder).

10. **Sustained Success**—Time-tested improvement tools to combat complacency and ensure lasting success (Treasure 10, Intentionally Improve, Marie Curie).

What's In Ten Treasures For You?

Big Ideas & Solutions. *Ten Treasures* challenges you to think critically and big. It asks the right questions (better questions lead to better answers). It steers you to think through the right issues, identify the right problems, and discover the right answers. The Treasures lead you to attain solutions that provide sustainable competitive advantage and accelerated value creation. They help organizations make a positive difference by creating better products and services, generating jobs, reducing waste, and providing more for philanthropy and stewardship.

New Approaches. The *Strategic Playbook* offers unique tools and new leadership techniques. These include the CURVE, dream-statement, TRUE goal, gravity-shifts, 3-Keys-Strategy, value chain breakthroughs, 5 Steps to Successful Succession, Yes, No, & Gray Zones, TEAMS[2] guidelines, and the Platinum Standard, among others. The *Strategic Playbook* also leverages important time-tested concepts including 80/20, Lean, OKRs, continuous improvement...

Proven, How-To Advice. The *Playbook* provides practical advice that you can turn into immediate action. I have personally implemented and validated the Playbook's wisdom in over fifty organizations (as CEO of three companies and as a direct advisor with the others).

Engaging Stories. The *Treasures* are revealed in a unique and engaging story format through ten highly successful sages from different time frames, countries, and circumstances. All have influenced world events. Each enhances the main idea of their respective chapter. The sages provide interest, relevance, and perspective.

Shareable Knowledge. The *Playbook* has easy to transfer ideas for transformative change. It rallies teams around a common language, tools, and techniques that deliver exceptional results.

Who Will Benefit?

o Leadership, executive, and management teams who seek a better way and would like a *strategic playbook* to guide them to success.
o Professionals who have a thirst to learn, advance, and become highly effective.
o Family businesses that want to successfully transfer their businesses to the next generations.
o Entrepreneurs who want to realize their dreams.
o Peer-learning organization members who prefer to work smarter, not just harder.
o Advisors, board members, and consultants who have a passion to see their clients succeed.
o Non-profit organizations who want to significantly improve value to service and donor customers by applying unique business wisdom.

There are two main characters in the book. Elizabeth Schulte is the new president. Her curious mind and strong leadership skills are put to the test in a struggling company she unexpectedly inherits. Joseph Powell is the strategist. He has an unusual and highly effective approach to teaching business success.

Three aligned and focused methods are used to clearly communicate the knowledge in the *Playbook*. The first features the unusual collection of ten highly successful sages. They introduce and reinforce the key points of each chapter. The second approach uses dialogue between Elizabeth and Joseph in which the right questions are asked and specific acronyms, diagrams, illustrations, and other *Playbook* examples are shared. Lastly, concise, high-level summaries are provided at the end of each Treasure.

Join Elizabeth and Joseph on their adventures traveling back in time. Learn as they personally visit ten sages at historically defining moments in their lives. Discover timeless treasures, principles, and advice that lead to healthy, enduring, and extraordinary businesses—enterprises that add value to and hopefully change our world for the better.

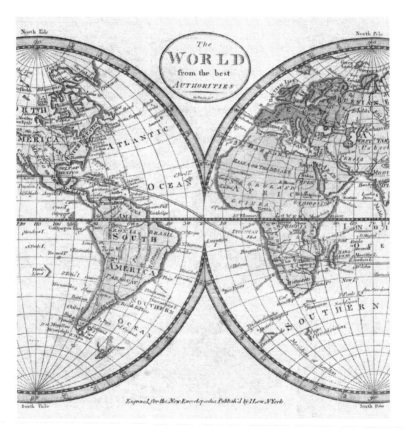

World Map by John Payne (1798)

PROLOGUE

SEEKING TREASURE

Elizabeth feels heaviness in her heart from the loss of her dad. While she is thankful that her beloved father left the business to her, she can't help asking: "Why did he leave the business in such poor financial shape?"

Earlier this morning, she met with Peak Precision Parts' (PPP's) bank. They are renegotiating PPP's loan agreement. The terms are not favorable. What's more, since she is now the largest shareholder, the bank is requesting personal guarantees from Elizabeth. That means her assets, including her home, can be in jeopardy. Elizabeth has little choice. She must accept the bank's upper-handed terms.

Elizabeth reflects on how, at age forty-two, she got into this predicament. PPP was founded by her father. He saw a need for quality manufacturing of precision parts for the medical industry. The company experienced growth and prosperity for over thirty years. That began to change when the recession turned things for the worse. A slow economic recovery and price competition from overseas significantly eroded revenues and more importantly, financial performance. In recent years, PPP has been taking on less profitable, more generic business to cover overhead.

Ready, Willing, & Able?

When her father suddenly passed, there was no succession plan. PPP did not have a ready, willing, and able candidate for the presidency. Through restless nights and deep discussions with family, friends, and PPP employees,

Elizabeth weighed the pros and cons of her choosing the leadership position at Peak Precision Parts.

On the one hand, Elizabeth thrived in situations where she had to learn quickly and lead. These traits and her ability to effectively respond to complex situations contributed to her unprecedented success in hospital administration. After going back to get her master's in nursing science at IU, she kept getting promoted to higher positions. To top it off, Elizabeth became the youngest ever Chief Nursing Officer at a highly-respected Indianapolis hospital. She was responsible for over 1,800 healthcare professionals and reported directly to the hospital's CEO. Elizabeth's strategic thinking, problem solving, and leadership skills, helped her advance.

On the other hand, Elizabeth knew that Peak Precision Parts had problems. Even though she had a lot of leadership and management experience, she acknowledged that she needed help to fix the company.

Financially, she had the most to gain and lose. But there was more to consider than money. It was the 578 Peak Precision Parts employees and their families. It was the community. For four decades, Peak Precision Parts had given significantly to local charities in the form of the three M's (Mind, Money, and Muscle). It was the legacy of a business which might not be around for a second-generation. It might not celebrate its Golden Jubilee. These were the tipping points.

Elizabeth recently resigned from her position at the hospital. She is the new president of PPP. She is in the hot seat. She must learn quickly and make smart decisions.

After Elizabeth made the decision to become president of PPP, she joined the National Association of Women Business Owners, an organization that propels growth and success for women-owned businesses. She also joined

Young President's Organization (YPO), a peer learning organization.

Elizabeth ponders potential solutions to her dilemma: "I need to find the right person to teach and guide me." She continues, "OK, who is that person?"

Timing is good. She has a YPO forum meeting tomorrow. Elizabeth's forum is made up of executives from nine different organizations. It is a good place to network and find the right person to guide her.

The next day, she shares her dilemma with the forum. Dave, the forum moderator, sums up her situation. "Elizabeth, you have the thirst to learn, the drive, and the leadership skills to turn around PPP. From what I've heard you say, you need Joseph Powell."

How Do You Win Monopoly?

Elizabeth and the Peak Precision Parts' leadership team have been meeting with and interviewing potential strategic consultants. Today, they are talking to Joseph Powell. Towards the conclusion of their meeting, Joseph asks Elizabeth an unexpected question. "How do you win the game of Monopoly?"

She replies, "You buy monopolies, then build on them." Joseph probes the next layer. "Which monopoly is your first preference?" She replies. "The blues: Boardwalk and Park Place." Joseph says in a non-emotional tone that he would like to play her in Monopoly. "I will most likely win but not because of luck. Rather, I will pursue a different monopoly." Her curiosity peaked, she asks, "Which one?" Joseph responds, "One on the opposite side of the board—the orange monopoly (New York, Tennessee, and Saint James Place)."

"Why the orange monopoly?" Joseph replies, "They are landed on the most. Among the forty locations on the board, Jail (visiting or otherwise) is landed on more than any other location. That's because if you roll doubles, you go to Jail. If you land on the opposite corner square (Go To Jail), it sends you directly to Jail (past the blues). If you select a Chance card, it can send you directly to Jail — again, past the blues. Coming from Jail, a roll of six, eight, or nine (a 39% probability) lands you on the orange monopoly."

After pausing and sensing that Elizabeth wants to learn more, Joseph continues. "Another advantage for orange is that there are three, not two properties...that in itself gives you a 50% advantage of being landed on over the blues."

The room is quiet. Even though Joseph has provided detailed facts and information, everyone is curious. They have all played Monopoly. They are absorbing the information. Joseph continues, "As to your response to the original question, you mentioned that you will build. That's an important tactic. The optimal investment is three houses per property. The orange properties require a lower optimal investment: $900 instead of $1,200 for the blues."

Joseph changes to a coaching style as he makes his last point. "Most people unwisely perceive that the blue monopoly is best (Boardwalk and Park Place are the most expensive properties; therefore, they must be best). Not many know that the orange monopoly is better than the blue. This insight makes it easier to trade for orange, especially if you have blue to trade.

"So, there are multiple advantages that exist with the game's design, the dice, and opportunities available because of false perceptions. Many who play Monopoly do not study the game or players to gain wisdom. They don't discover the advantages that increase the odds for success."

Elizabeth learns a valuable lesson. Namely, most people pick the wrong monopoly because they do not think strategically about how to win the game. They just play, react, and let the dice determine their fate.

Joseph makes the point that like winning in Monopoly, success in business is about taking the dice out of the game as much as possible by leveraging insights to obtain a unique competitive advantage. It's about making conscious and intentional strategic choices. It's about solving problems and figuring out how to win more and lose less.

Elizabeth turns to Joseph and says, "I like your term *unique competitive advantage*. It prompts me to ask why Peak Precision Parts should engage you…what is unique about your approach?"

Joseph replies, "Good question. I think anyone you strongly consider must have a 'basket-of-givens.' This can include attributes: high-integrity; good communication and listening skills; a passion to help; proven experience; and good chemistry. As to my unique approach, three things come to mind."

Teaching Treasures

Joseph shares the first of three unique advantages. "First are Teaching Treasures. Any worthy advisor must teach you how to think more strategically so you become more successful. As the proverb goes, teach you how to fish instead of handing you fish. This ensures lessons are owned by leadership, transferable to others, and sustainable long after I'm gone.

"One way I teach you to think more strategically is by telling stories. This time-tested technique draws you in and activates the whole brain. Stories help you emotionally live the experience. They provide knowledge about how to act and emotional inspiration to act.

"Historical legends are featured in the stories to illustrate important success principles. Many of these legends (sages) did not have modern day business backgrounds. What they did have was plenty of experience directly related to the strategic principle being taught. They are treasures, full of wisdom." He adds a related point. "You will also hear appropriate quotes and anecdotes that concisely reinforce the stories and strategic principles."

Elizabeth asks, "How have clients responded?" Joseph replies, "Clients consistently say the Teaching Treasures improve engagement, learning, and recall...the lessons take root."

The Right Questions

He continues. "The second point of uniqueness is asking The Right Questions. Better questions lead to better results. It takes experience and reflection to know what questions to ask, when to ask them, and how to ask them. Over time, I have learned what, when, and how to ask The Right Questions.

"All questions are carefully worded to help you think through the right issues, identify the right problems, and discover the right answers. They invite participation. They remind people where to focus and look. They penetrate to the heart of the matter. They trigger insights, fresh ideas, and solutions that work."

Elizabeth asks, "Can you answer the questions if you are not very familiar with the business?" He replies, "Most people are intelligent enough to answer the questions correctly—especially if the questions relate to their personal business scenarios. They just need to be prompted with the right questions. All that is needed are sincere and thoughtful responses.

"There is a side benefit of this approach; there is more ownership when you discover solutions through your own answers. The *'How do you win Monopoly'* question is a case in point. That question led to quick understanding of how to strategically play the game of business. That's the power of asking The Right Questions."

Strategic Playbook

Joseph continues, "The last point of uniqueness is the Strategic Playbook. Having traveled into the inner workings of many organizations through strategic planning, hands-on work, and board advisory service, I've uncovered keys to excellence.

"Real life examples help you discover superior solutions. Clients have found the keys to excellence contained within the Strategic Playbook pick up the pace of learning, sharing, and successful implementation. The use of unique communication tools helps to transfer knowledge and realize success."

The Unique Choice

Elizabeth and the leadership team have narrowed it to three strategic planning candidates. They have completed reference checks. They are discussing who they will use to help them turn around PPP and rebuild a great company. There is agreement that all candidates are a reasonably good fit in terms of Joseph's *basket-of-givens*. However, Joseph was the most unique with his Teaching Treasures, The Right Questions, and Strategic Playbook.

Steve, the Peak Precision Parts' CFO, brings forth a positive point. "Joseph asked more questions about us than the other consultants. It appeared that Joseph wanted to ensure there would be a win-win relationship."

Art, the head of sales provides another point, "You know what they say about common sense, it's not a gift, it's a punishment because you still must deal with everyone around you who doesn't have it. For my money, I like Joseph's practical, easy to share approach."

Markus, the director of human resources, adds a final comment. "Joseph looked beyond the immediate business. Several of his 'right questions' helped connect the business to making a positive difference in the world. This resonates with me personally."

With respect to references, in a nutshell, Joseph has a sterling reputation. He was described as "possessing a true gift of teaching the right strategic principles to successfully build a lasting business...one that makes a difference."

The decision is made. Elizabeth hires Joseph to teach them how to turn around the company and get them on a path towards success. After getting alignment on outcomes and other details, they mutually agree on a working arrangement.

Next Steps

Joseph says that he will be sending a comprehensive survey that has a series of Competitive Comparison Questions and open-ended Discovery Questions. "These are to be filled out by all fifty-five managers and leaders within the organization. After receiving survey results, I will conduct one-on-one interviews with the leadership team. I will review the financials and important internal documents. This initial assessment will point us to specific strategic areas that need improvement."

Elizabeth asks, "How will we work on the strategic plan?" Joseph responds, "I will prepare for and lead a series of offsite meetings. In those meetings, I will engage the leadership team in strategic exercises, provide examples of excellence from the Strategic Playbook, and continue to ask The Right Questions. The goal is to help you discover and own the solutions that will enable PPP to be successful long-term."

First Offsite Meeting

Everyone from the leadership team believes that Joseph asked terrific questions in the surveys and one-on-one meetings. According to Lisa (VP of Operations), "The questions made you think strategically about the business, its customers, competition, products, priorities, employees, unique competitive advantages...Joseph did a good job of setting the stage. The wheels of strategic improvement are circling in our minds."

It's 7:50 AM on a Thursday. Elizabeth and the Peak Precision Parts' leadership team are in an offsite meeting facility in Indianapolis. There is a sense of excitement. Everyone is hopeful that these offsite meetings will lead to a healthy recovery.

The attendees have finished their continental breakfast. Most are seated around a large U-shaped table. The highly awaited first strategic session is about to begin.

To Elizabeth's surprise, Joseph has not arrived. Concerned, Elizabeth starts pacing. The meeting is supposed to start at 8:00 AM. She goes out and looks in the lobby. No Joseph. Elizabeth asks the meeting facility receptionist. No word from Joseph.

Elizabeth asks herself, "Did we get our days, times, or locations mixed up?" She checks prior emails. Every correspondence clearly says Thursday with an 8:00 AM start at this location.

Elizabeth calls Joseph several times on his cell. There is no answer. She tries text messages and emails. No reply. After attempting to contact Joseph multiple times, Elizabeth decides to cancel the offsite meeting. All the references said he was responsible and diligent. She is disappointed.

As she is driving back to PPP's headquarters, Elizabeth hits unexpected traffic getting on to the northbound entrance to the highway. Everyone is rubber necking. Southbound lanes are completely shut down. Elizabeth is glad she is not heading south. She sees two crushed cars, multiple police cars, and firetrucks. She hears an ambulance leaving the scene. Elizabeth thinks to herself, "That's a serious accident. They are probably headed to my old hospital. I hope everyone is okay."

News Flash

During her lunch break, Elizabeth looks on her cell phone and reads a local news flash:

> *The Indiana State Highway Patrol reported that during the early morning rush hour, there was a tragic accident. An Indianapolis man was killed*

when his vehicle was struck by another driver going the wrong way on I-65. One of the vehicles overturned and caught fire.

Elizabeth says to herself, "I saw that accident." Then it hits her. Could the auto accident she witnessed in the morning be Joseph? Shocked, she learns it was. He was on his way to their meeting when he was killed.

Words of Love

Several days later, Elizabeth gets a gut feeling: go to the funeral. As she walks into the church, she notices there is a big turnout. She sits in a pew. Moments later, Jane Powell, Joseph's wife, gives his eulogy:

> "I miss him so much." Jane pauses as she pulls herself together. "I really appreciate the outpouring of love and support received from all of you.
>
> "Joseph was special...to me, our family, and everyone who met him. He could engage an audience, small or large, with his story telling and wit, or make them laugh with his charming humor. Joseph also had a sensitive side that could be misunderstood. One had to look beyond the intensity and see that it was his curious mind just acting in a fast, mindful way. His direct approach was his courageous honesty. I admired his sensitivity to everything and how he acted the same with everyone.
>
> "Joseph and I have signed our cards to each other for as long as I can remember with these words; 'Love always...and...in all ways.' This is an example of his beautifully simple expressions coming from his sensitive special self.

"Joseph's path through life was one of true love and devotion. I loved how he loved our children and me. He walked with me, talked with me, felt with me, and loved with me.

"So, my loving Joseph, until I see you again. See yourself as ageless because of all the things that you did and went through. Remember yourself as timeless because of all the boundaries that you have crossed. And treasure yourself as priceless because of the characteristics that you possessed that no amount of money could have bought."

Leaving the funeral, Elizabeth feels a sense of loss. She would have enjoyed working with such a good person.

A Playbook with a CURVE

It's a Sunday evening. It's been over a week since Joseph's funeral. Elizabeth is doing the dishes after a quick dinner at home. She hears the doorbell ring. She goes to open the door. Unexpectedly, Jane Powell is standing under the porch light. Jane is holding a large package.

Elizabeth invites her inside. Jane says to Elizabeth, "I was going through Joseph's business affairs and came across this. I think it may be useful to you." Elizabeth comforts Jane with a warm hug. Elizabeth says she is praying for her. They smile at each other as Jane leaves.

Sitting in her family room leather chair, Elizabeth opens the package with anticipation. She looks over a lengthy, comprehensive, and intriguing PowerPoint presentation. It is titled: *Ten Treasures Strategic Playbook*.

Elizabeth realizes that this is Joseph's complete teaching and facilitation guide for his strategic consulting engagement with Peak Precision Parts. It contains stories, questions, diagrams, illustrations, examples, acronyms, quotes, and survey results. It covers Ten Treasures (strategic topics) he planned to teach Elizabeth and her leadership team.

Elizabeth starts reading the presentation. She is particularly interested in three things she sees within the Playbook: a value equation called the CURVE, PPP's Competitive Comparison Questions survey results, and a diagram that shows how to think about the Ten Treasures.

The CURVE

The CURVE is a value-equation that Joseph created using an acronym (Customer Unique and Relative Value Equation). Elizabeth notices an illustration comparing a weak and strong CURVE and how they relate to the right strategic direction:

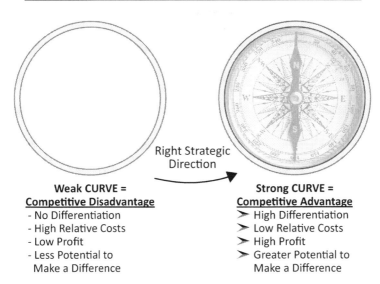

Customer Unique and Relative Value Equation (CURVE)

Right Strategic Direction

Weak CURVE =
Competitive Disadvantage
- No Differentiation
- High Relative Costs
- Low Profit
- Less Potential to
  Make a Difference

Strong CURVE =
Competitive Advantage
➤ High Differentiation
➤ Low Relative Costs
➤ High Profit
➤ Greater Potential to
  Make a Difference

The CURVE is showcased throughout the *Ten Treasures Strategic Playbook*. Joseph provided commentary on how the CURVE is linked to profit, competitive advantage, and strategy:

"A key outcome of business success is long-term profitability. On the one hand, if you don't have profits, it's difficult to survive long term. On the other hand, if you have strong profitability, many positive outcomes and choices accrue.

"Linking strategy to profitability is deceptively simple. It starts with a value equation I call the CURVE (Customer Unique and Relative Value Equation). The equation has a top and a bottom part (numerator and denominator). It is defined as follows:

"Value = what customers uniquely and relatively get (top part, the numerator), divided by what customers relatively pay (bottom part, the denominator). Value must be meaningful and different as perceived by the customer. It is always relative to other customer choices.

"Let's review the CURVE illustration. When you have a weak CURVE (left side of the illustration), the organization is unhealthy and lacks strategic direction. There is competitive *disadvantage*. There is no differentiation. Products and services are commodities. Costs are relatively high. Profits are low or nonexistent. Wages tend to be low. There is less potential to make a difference in the world. Value-add activities such as giving back to communities are compromised.

"When you have a strong CURVE (right side of the illustration), there is strong competitive advantage and strategic direction. Differentiation is high. Products and services are unique, meaningful, and superior. Costs are relatively low. Profits and wages tend to be high. More profit increases the potential for the organization to create jobs and prosperity for people…to reduce waste…to provide more for giving back. There is greater potential to make a positive difference in the world.

"While the CURVE implies that strategy is simple, nothing can be further from the truth. Successful strategy is complex. Good strategy involves all activities a company pursues—on the top and bottom parts of the value equation.

"Good strategy is about making the right, focused yet connected choices of what to do and what *not to do*. Purposely make smart choices that magnify your competitive advantages—that make you unique and difficult to copy.

"It's the cumulative impact of making the right, connected strategic choices that create meaningful differences in what customers uniquely and relatively get (top part or numerator) divided by what they relatively pay (bottom part or denominator). Those choices improve the CURVE. They drive true competitive advantage. They deliver superior profit."

Elizabeth thinks to herself, "This is a different way of looking at business strategy from what I recently read in top selling business books." She is absorbing the information but is not sure how to apply it yet. It's a lot to take in. She continues to read. When she sees a familiar reference to Monopoly, something she learned firsthand from Joseph, it makes more sense:

"As we learn in playing simple games like Monopoly, business success is mainly about finding unique and meaningful advantages. If your CURVE is weak, the dice take over. Your chances for long-term success are not very good. You want unique strategic advantages that are not obvious to your competitors — advantages that are difficult for competition to copy.

"If you want to be more successful (profitable), make wise decisions that strengthen your CURVE. The good news is that there are three primary choices to strengthen your CURVE. First, you can improve the top part of the CURVE (what customers uniquely and relatively get). You do this by creating and improving your unique offerings (to satisfy customer needs) versus other customer choices. This enables you to earn a premium price and therefore, higher profit.

"Second, you can focus on improving the bottom part of the CURVE (what customers relatively pay). You do this by reducing your costs relative to competition. This is all about using your resources wisely and effectively. Reducing costs relative to competition enables you to earn more profit and offer more overall value.

"Third, and this approach is strongly recommended, you can pursue a combination of the previous two choices. Most successful strategies and companies work on improving the top and bottom parts of the CURVE."

Elizabeth rereads that sentence: "*Most successful strategies and companies work on improving the top and bottom parts of the CURVE.*"

In the Playbook, Elizabeth sees a diagram that visualizes the importance of working the top and bottom parts of the CURVE. It shows how doing that will result in higher profit:

CURVE
Customer Unique and Relative Value Equation

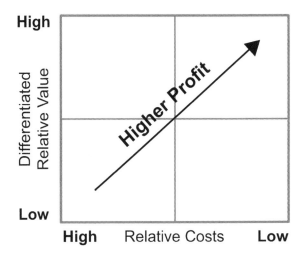

Elizabeth continues to read about the CURVE. "Successful strategy is about strengthening the CURVE. That's because it is linked to competitive advantage and earning more profit. Remember, if you have true competitive advantage, you will earn higher profits than the industry norm."

Ten Lowest
Competitive Comparison Survey Results

Another point of keen interest to Elizabeth in the *Ten Treasures Strategic Playbook* is the summary results of PPP's ten lowest scoring Competitive Comparison Questions.

As part of the strategic planning process, Joseph fielded a Competitive Comparison Questions survey. The questions asked Peak Precision Parts' fifty-five managers and leaders to respond using a five-point rating scale. A rating of "1" is significantly worse than competition. A rating of "5" is significantly better than competition. A rating of "3" is equal to competition.

These results show the average scores and indexes of all fifty-five managers and leaders who took the survey. The ten lowest are presented in rank from lowest to highest.

The scores are troubling to Elizabeth. In eight of ten categories, PPP scored lower than its perceived competition:

Peak Precision Parts (PPP) Competitive Comparison Questions (Responses from 55 surveys, relative to competition)	Average (All Ratings) *	Index (100 = 3.0) **	Rank (Low to High)
How clearly defined is PPP's future?	1.4	47	1
How would you rate PPP's innovation abilities and strategies?	1.7	56	2
How well does PPP identify, attract, hire, and retain the right top talent?	2.1	70	3
How effectively do PPP's operational disciplines lower costs and improve competitive advantage?	2.3	75	4
How well does PPP prioritize (focus on the important, say no to the less important)?	2.3	78	5
How appropriate is PPP's pace of growth?	2.4	80	6
How unique and meaningful is PPP's value position?	2.5	83	7
How well defined and healthy is PPP's culture?	2.6	85	8
How simple and easy-to-do work are PPP's work flow and structure?	3.0	100	9
How well does PPP intentionally improve its systems and processes?	3.1	103	10

* 5 point scale where: "1" is significantly worse than competition; "2" is directionally worse than competition; "3" is equal to competition; "4" is directionally better than competition; and "5" is significantly better than competition. ** Index to Competition. 3.0 = 100.

How To Think About The Ten Treasures

The next item that catches Elizabeth's interest in the Strategic Playbook is a visual of how to think about the Ten Treasures:

Ten Connected Treasures

She reads Joseph's brief commentary:

"The Ten Treasures can be useful to any organization that wants to add value to and change our world for the better. The Treasures apply to manufacturing, service, and merchandising companies. They are relevant for family, entrepreneurial, and professionally managed enterprises. Most of the Treasures can be used in non-profit organizations.

"The Ten Treasures are connected. Four of the Treasures provide the strategic foundation: Define The Dream (Treasure 1), Niche The New (Treasure 2), Tap The Top Talent (Treasure 3), and Operational Discipline: Helps You Win (Treasure 4). Every Treasure is strategic. However, these four are the essential paths to superior strategy. They are the focal points—the keys to competitive advantage and building a strong CURVE. You must get these right in order to succeed over time.

"While all Treasures positively impact profit, three are strong profit accelerators: Elevate The Elephants (Treasure 5), Pace The Growth (Treasure 6), and Unique Position: A

Better Decision (Treasure 7). More profit means greater potential to make a difference.

"Cultivate a Healthy Culture (Treasure 8) and Make Work Simple (Treasure 9) provide the cultural foundation. It's important that these culturally focused Treasures are developed in concert with strategy. Too many organizations isolate culture from strategy. This is a missed opportunity.

"Intentionally Improve (Treasure 10) overlays every Treasure. It is the sustainability enhancer. Organizations that intentionally improve, live longer, heathier lives."

Midnight Dreams

Elizabeth thinks to herself, "My competitors would pay a lot to get their hands on this." She realizes that the *Playbook* is a valuable treasure map. It charts a path of where and how to succeed. However, it does not have the in-the-moment interaction and insightful follow-up discussion that Joseph would have provided. Elizabeth wishes Joseph was alive to help her lead and guide the company to a better future.

As Elizabeth continues to read the *Ten Treasures Strategic Playbook*, time flows quickly. From the entrance hall in her home, she hears her grandfather clock strike twelve times. It is midnight. Elizabeth falls asleep. She drifts into a dream…

Elizabeth sees Joseph. Surprised by his appearance, she asks, "What are you doing in my dream?" Joseph smiles and says, "Let's go on a journey." Elizabeth hesitates then asks, "Where are we going?"

Joseph replies, "To seek treasure."

TREASURE

1

DEFINE THE DREAM

Elizabeth finds herself outside walking amongst a large crowd. People of all races and ages are alongside. Many are dressed in their Sunday best. They are carrying signs and singing in unison, "We shall overcome someday."

Elizabeth notices Joseph walking at her side. She asks him, "What do you mean we are going to seek treasure?" As she looks around, she realizes they are approaching the Washington Mall. Joseph responds, "We are in the March on Washington for Jobs and Freedom. We are taking a dream-journey back in time. Today is August 28, 1963." As they proceed on the march, she asks Joseph, "Are we really going to see Dr. Martin Luther King Jr.?"

Connections

People keep filling up the mall. There are 250,000 in attendance. Elizabeth and Joseph arrive at their destination. They are standing on the gray granite steps of the Lincoln Memorial. Elizabeth is struck by the juxtaposition of two facts. It is 100 years after Lincoln issued the Emancipation Proclamation. King will be speaking directly in front of the Lincoln statue. It is situated above the podium in the alcove at the top of the steps.

Elizabeth perks up when she hears the introduction. "At this time, I have the honor to present to you the moral leader of our nation." King begins his sixteen-minute oration. He refers to the Emancipation Proclamation given by President Lincoln. He echoes the words of the

Gettysburg Address. "Five score years ago." King goes on to weave emotional imagery. He connects with the crowd. He paints a vivid picture of the despair and pain that African Americans face. He describes the lack of freedoms, segregation, and discrimination of the day. He acknowledges the difficulties. He clearly states that they must be faced. King's words touch Elizabeth's heart.

Tell 'Em About The Dream

At one point, Elizabeth hears the gospel singer, Mahalia Jackson, call out, *"Tell 'em about the dream, Martin."* After Jackson's request, Elizabeth senses that King goes off script. He seems to speak more deliberatively. His captivating orations pulse into the crowd. He paints a dream of a better, more remarkable future.

At the pinnacle of his speech, Elizabeth gets completely caught in the moment. King powerfully, persuasively, and repeatedly uses four historic words: "I have a dream." These words dramatize the emotional essence of King's message. King continues, "I have a dream, that one day this nation will rise up and live out the true meaning of its creed." At the speech's conclusion, Elizabeth has a strong sense of hope for the future of mankind.

The Mountaintop

Joseph breaks Elizabeth's thoughts and says, "We have another dream-journey to take." Elizabeth asks, "Where are we going?" Before Joseph can answer, she and Joseph are sitting in auditorium seats. It is an intimate setting. Joseph answers her question, "We are in the Bishop Charles Mason Temple in Memphis, Tennessee. We've dream-journeyed ahead almost five years to April 3, 1968. Dr. King is here in Memphis to support a strike of the city's African American sanitation workers." At that moment, King begins an impassioned speech. His words are fateful. He mentions uncertainty for the future.

He acknowledges that difficult days are still to come. King says he does not mind because, "I've been to the mountain top…I'm not fearing any man. Mine eyes have seen the glory of the coming of the Lord."

Go Back Inside

Joseph and Elizabeth dream journey forward to another destination. Joseph drives Elizabeth to a parking lot. They are at the Lorraine Motel in Memphis, Tennessee. As they get out of the car, Elizabeth looks at her watch…it is 6:00 PM. She sees Dr. King standing on a second story balcony. Elizabeth asks Joseph, "What day was MLK assassinated?" Joseph replies, "April 4." Elizabeth's instincts take charge. She starts running and shouts to King, "Go back inside. Please, get back inside!"

Before she can reach Dr. King, they dream-journey to Elizabeth's home. Elizabeth says, "I feel so helpless. If only he could have heard me." Joseph replies, "You are here to learn and find treasure, not to change fate." Elizabeth replies, "My emotions are cross-firing. His speech was so uplifting and inspirational. On the other hand, his death was horrific. I don't get this 'seeking treasure' thing."

Joseph responds, "Martin Luther's 'I Have a Dream' speech clearly articulated a future free of discrimination and segregation. It is a great speech on positive change. King described his dream of freedom and equality arising from a land of slavery and hatred. He captured why the future will be better, more remarkable. He defined his dream. He caught the world's attention. Through his life and death, King changed the world."

Defining a Dream with FATE

Joseph transitions to business. "Having worked with many businesses in a variety of industries over many years, it is not surprising to find that the area PPP needs the most improvement in is *providing greater clarity for where the business is headed*. As you know from seeing the survey results of the Competitive Comparison Questions, the question, 'How clearly defined is PPP's future, relative to competition,' scored the lowest.

"To refresh your memory, the Competitive Comparison Questions were not meant to represent a scientific or precise comparison of your company to competition. They were simply trying to identify, based on internal management perceptions, which areas need the most improvement for PPP to be successful. Looking at this low score, the leadership team has an important opportunity to clarify its future direction.

"So, let's talk about how to improve the score. More importantly, let's learn from Dr. Martin Luther King, Jr. Let's define a clearer, better future for Peak Precision Parts.

"Organizations are a collection of people with various degrees of energy and talent. One of leadership's primary jobs is to focus that energy and talent. Effective leadership sets a clear direction that leads to a better future. It connects daily and long-term activities. It leads by providing the right strategic compass.

"One of the exciting things about working in an organization is being part of something bigger than yourself—being on a transformative journey to create something remarkable...to make a difference in the world...pursuing a dream that you comprehend and buy into."

Turning Vague Definitions Into Good Dreams

Joseph continues, "There are options, varying definitions, and confusion as to what to use to guide a company to success. Unlike Dr. Martin Luther King Jr.'s dream, many organizations have vague, cluttered, convoluted vision, mission, and purpose statements. They do not inspire positive change. Too often, these documents provide a weak strategic compass for the path forward."

Elizabeth comments, "I am uncertain what the different statements mean." Joseph replies. "You are not alone. The problem stems from a lack of universally accepted definitions."

Elizabeth asks Joseph, "Do you recommend separate or multiple statements?" Joseph advises, "I recommend that you and your leadership team create a single statement—a Peak Precision Parts' dream-statement. It combines the best elements of mission, vision, and purpose statements into one simple, yet more strategic and future oriented statement. Let's start with a definition:

> 'A dream-statement is a strategic, aspirational, easy-to-grasp description of a more remarkable, better future state of an organization. Its intent is to achieve long-term success by improving strategic guidance, alignment, and commitment.'

"A good dream-statement does a better job of teaching strategy (how to build and preserve competitive advantage) than typical vision, purpose, or mission statements.

"A good dream-statement captures the human spirit to go beyond current possibilities. It embraces tomorrow. It portrays a *more remarkable, better future*. It is more powerful and aspirational than typical statements."

Joseph recommends, "Having one statement can improve communication. It can provide better strategic guidance, alignment, and help achieve long-term success. It accomplishes these important outcomes if it is crisp, focused, and carefully crafted. It should not try to be everything to everyone."

Joseph continues, "To build a great business, it helps to have the right strategic compass—to define what direction to work towards. We witnessed how Dr. Martin Luther King Jr. was able to inspire a better future for segregation and discrimination in his mesmerizing *I Have A Dream* speech. Successful organizations work towards a better tomorrow. The dream-statement is a useful tool to help you define and get to a better future."

Elizabeth asks, "Do you have any tips that can help Peak Precision Parts create a good dream-statement?"

Joseph answers, "Yes, here are dream-statement guidelines from the Strategic Playbook. A good dream-statement follows FATE." Joseph hands Elizabeth the FATE guidelines:

Dream-Statement FATE Guidelines

Future Dream:
o   Vividly bring into focus a remarkable future dream that is materially better than the current reality.
o   Define a future beyond just profit. Answer how the company is going to make a positive difference in the world, in part by focusing on making lives better.
o   Be powerful and aspirational to motivate transformative change. Leveraging genuine emotion can improve the power of a dream-statement.

Align:
o   Excite, unite, and align the organization behind a better future.
o   Align with the company's culture and values.
o   Reflect motivations for doing the organization's great work, thereby driving buy-in and commitment.

Teach Strategy:

o   Teach how the organization aspires to build and preserve competitive advantage.
o   Incorporate what is unique about the strategy.
o   Guide virtually everything in the company.

Easy to Share:

o   Ensure the dream-statement is easy to communicate and share (both internally and externally).
o   Be specific, clear, and concise. Specificity in language is important. Words and language matter.
o   The dream-statement should be written (pictures and videos can be used, if helpful).

Poor Vision

Joseph continues to teach Elizabeth how to create a useful dream-statement. "Many organizations provide a murky picture of the future." Joseph shows Elizabeth a real picture of a group of distracting street signs and asks a rhetorical question. "Can you imagine trying to get some place and seeing this group of signs at an intersection along the highway?"

Joseph continues, "Sadly, complicated signs within organizations are too common." Joseph makes an important point. "When you see a company with a confusing vision, purpose, or mission statement, you tend to find mediocre or poor performance. Said another way, if you are unclear where you are headed, any road will get you there."

Joseph pulls out a piece of paper with a vision statement printed on it:

> "Peak Precision Parts' vision is to be the best. We manufacture, distribute, and service world-class precision products for the medical industry. We care about our customers. We believe the customer is always right. As such, we seek to exceed their expectations. We value integrity and honesty. We also believe good communication to all employees is essential. We treat employees with respect and seek to provide a high-quality and fair work environment for all our employees. We constantly strive to make products that are the highest quality. Quality is essential—it is our highest priority. As a demonstration of our ongoing commitment to quality, we are ISO 13485 certified. Safety is also job number one for everyone at our company. We believe in good citizenship. We support good works and charitable giving in the communities in which we live and work. We strive to satisfy stakeholder interests and provide a good return for shareholders."

Joseph asks Elizabeth, "What do you think about this statement?" She responds, "My father, with input from the entire company, put that together. It's like your street-signs picture. It gives a lot of information, yet it does not give clear-cut strategic direction. It attempts to cover too much. While it has good principles and statements, it's not very inspirational. Let's see, what else…it doesn't bring into focus a more remarkable future that is materially better than the current state." Joseph smiles as he replies, "You are clearly getting the picture."

Joseph adds a criticism. "It talks about being the best. Typically, that does not drive a unique competitive advantage. It often leads to a win or lose approach to business. It often leads to an unprofitable race to the bottom with me-too products and services. It is wiser to focus on strategically unique areas where you add value. We will discuss this in depth later."

Joseph offers another critique. "It intermingles values into the vision statement. This adds clutter and potential confusion. Better to have the values listed separately, alongside, or perhaps underneath the statement. We will discuss how to create effective values later."

A Social Media Dream

Joseph asks Elizabeth if she uses social media. She responds, "Yes, selectively and infrequently." Joseph asks, "Why don't you use social media more often?" She responds, "I am concerned about privacy." From his Strategic Playbook, Joseph hands Elizabeth an example of a fictitious social media company dream-statement:

> "Founded by three entrepreneurs in 1999, our dream is to provide users with the power to connect with anyone in the world, to build community, and to bring everyone closer together. Our platform is used to communicate with family and friends, to learn what's happening in our world, and to provide a voice to our users so they can express what is important to them."

Joseph asks Elizabeth what she thinks. After thinking it over, she responds, "I would not give it a high grade." Joseph agrees and says, "Let's discuss how this statement fairs based on the FATE guidelines."

Future Dream?

Joseph asks, "What is the better, more remarkable future dream?" Elizabeth responds, "I don't know. It basically describes existing social media platforms." Joseph replies, "I agree. Is it very compelling, aspirational, emotional?" Elizabeth answers, "Yes, I like the words, *'provide users with the power to connect with anyone in the world, to build community, and to bring everyone closer together.'*"

Align?

Joseph asks, "How well does it build commitment?" Elizabeth replies, "I think it aligns the organization behind the current social media market. However, it does not align towards a better future." Joseph concurs with Elizabeth.

Teach Strategy?

Joseph says, "Let's try interchanging actual social media platforms such as Twitter, Facebook, YouTube, and Instagram into our hypothetical dream-statement." After doing this for each platform, Elizabeth comments, "That really shows that this dream-statement is not very unique." Joseph replies, "I agree, since it can apply to any of the existing companies, it does not effectively teach good strategy."

Easy to Share?

Joseph comments, "Only the essential words are in a good dream-statement. 'Founded by three entrepreneurs in 1999;' why complicate the statement with these extra words that do not appear to be strategic? Businesses live for the future. While we are on the topic, it isn't important to just eliminate words. There may be essential language to be added to a dream-statement."

Joseph asks Elizabeth if she can recall President Kennedy's speech about going to moon.

Elizabeth replies. "I believe it went something like, '*We will land a man on the moon before the end of the decade.*'" Encouragingly, Joseph says, "You got the first part right. Most people don't mention four important words: '*And return him safely.*'" Elizabeth replies, "I see your point. Language is important."

Joseph hands Elizabeth an alternative version of a fictitious social media company dream-statement:

> "Our dream: Create the *safest and most trustworthy* social media platform in the world. It will enable any user worldwide to connect, share ideas and emotions, and inspire more profoundly and inclusively than ever before."

Joseph asks for Elizabeth's reaction. She says, "I like it. It talks about a better, more remarkable future. It provides more strategic guidance. It sounds like a company that wants to place a strategic stake in *safety and trustworthiness* (privacy). It does not sound like a me-too company. I would be interested in this company." Joseph replies. "Excellent. The interesting thing is that this dream-statement provides clearer strategic direction but with fewer words; thirty-five versus sixty-five."

A TRUE Goal

Elizabeth asks Joseph for his thoughts on long-term goals to further improve clarity for the future direction of PPP. Joseph responds, "As we discussed, a dream-statement is analogous to the right compass points. It provides clearer strategic direction towards a better, more remarkable future beyond just profit. With that said, it is a good idea to focus on a future profit goal. Profit increases the potential for the organization to prosper, make a difference, and give back. A well thought out long-term goal is a sound way to do this.

"Many business executives and consultants use a BHAG ® (Big Hairy Audacious Goal), developed and trademarked by Jim Collins and Jerry Porras. Regardless what you call it, at its best, it is a top level, integrated long-term goal that drives and aligns the organization to a specific destination further out in the future. Think of it as the company's long-term and most important GPS coordinates.

"I use a TRUE acronym: **T**ied to Profit; **R**isk-aligned; **U**nmistakable; **E**xplosive."

Tied To Profit

Elizabeth asks about the first letter in the acronym, "T" (Tied-to-profit). "Why do you suggest that the TRUE goal be linked to profit?" Joseph responds with something she read in the Playbook related to the CURVE (Customer Unique and Relative Value Equation).

"A key outcome of business success is long-term profitability. If you have strong profitability, many positive choices accrue, all related to business success. Successful businesses have competitive advantages. They uniquely create superior customer value relative to competitive choices. In so doing, they earn the right to more profit than competition. More profit increases the potential for the organization to be a force for good…to create more jobs and prosperity for people…to reduce waste…to give back. That is why I recommend the TRUE goal be linked to a key measure of profitability. Profit is an essential measure of long-term business success. It enables the organization to add value to and change our world for the better."

Elizabeth asks Joseph, "What specific profit-based goals are good to consider for Peak Precision Parts' TRUE goal?" Joseph replies, "The old saying, '*what gets measured gets done*,' is valid. I like return on invested capital or return on human capital (people). They are excellent profit-based measures of how well an organization is effectively using its capital or people resources.

"Consider return on invested capital if you have high investments in capital. Consider return on invested human capital if you have high investments in people. If you have high investments in both, then consider both measures."

Joseph hands Elizabeth a Strategic Playbook list of profit goals (measures) to consider for PPP's TRUE goal:

Peak Precision Parts' TRUE Goal Profit Measure Considerations

o Net profit (margin or dollars).
o Return on invested capital (ROIC). To calculate, take the company's net income and subtract out all dividends. Divide this by the total capital invested in the business (i.e., net income – dividends *divided by* total capital).
o Return on invested human capital (ROIHC). To calculate, take the company's total revenues and subtract out all direct manufacturing costs, and all labor, salary, and benefit expenses. Divide this by the total of all labor, salary, and benefit expenses. Include all people investments such as part time, corporate overhead personnel, and outsourced labor.
o Earnings before interest, taxes, depreciation, and amortization (EBITDA).

Risk Factor

Joseph continues, "Let's talk about the letter 'R' (risk). A TRUE goal is a good way to stretch the organization to a better future. However, when executives' tolerances for risk are ignored, assumed, or unknown, a problematic long-term goal can be established. Typically, the leader with the most power, or the one with the most persuasive voice, sets an overly audacious or explosive goal. Sometimes the opposite happens and a low stretch (conservative) goal is set. Goals can be misaligned with members of the leadership team and stakeholders."

Elizabeth interjects. "I see your point, but isn't risk complicated?" Joseph replies, "Yes. The good news is that the Strategic Playbook has a 'vaguely-right' tool to assess risk tolerance. Many leadership teams have had excellent results using it. At a minimum, it helps everyone understand an important dynamic — namely, risk tolerance. Risk is a fundamental driver of people's motivations, behaviors, and decision-making dynamics."

Joseph hands Elizabeth the Risk Tolerance Continuum (and directions for use) from the Strategic Playbook:

Risk Tolerance Continuum

To better understand risk tolerances, ask each team member on the leadership or executive team to rate their risk tolerance, as it relates to the workplace. Have them use a one-to-ten scale. Explain that the lowest workplace-based risk tolerance would be denoted by the number '1' (ultra-risk adverse). On the other end of the scale, explain that the highest workplace-based tolerance for risk would be denoted with the number '10' (extreme, freewheeling, with virtually no concern for consequences). In the responses ask for a whole number from the lowest risk tolerance ('1') to the highest tolerance for risk ('10'). Remind the leadership team that there isn't a perfect measure for risk. Ask each person to rate and share their best guestimate.

Joseph comments. "Sharing risk assessments often leads to interesting discussion among team members. Sometimes responses are different than what you may otherwise surmise. Regardless, it is helpful to know the range (low to high) and the individual risk assessments.

"If your team has a tight range, say '6' to '8,' alignment on how audacious you set the TRUE goal can be relatively easy. If the team has a wide range, things get more interesting."

Unmistakable

"Unmistakable is straight forward. There should be no mistake as to what the goal is (specific), whether or not it is achieved (measurable), and by when it will be achieved (time bound). It must be clear, crisp, and easy to communicate."

Explosive

"Most organizations desire explosive growth. It ensures that the organization is going to truly stretch in its growth ambitions.

"Thinking big (explosive) is important to future success. Do not automatically take the average of the leadership team's risk assessments to set the stretch or explosiveness of the TRUE goal. Have the team discuss and agree on the audacity of the TRUE goal. Aligning what's best for the company, its owners, and other stakeholders is what's important. The tradeoffs between risk tolerance and explosiveness should be understood, discussed, and factored into the long-term goal, as appropriate."

Elizabeth comments: "I have another question. What about the time frame for the TRUE goal?" Joseph responds, "There is no formula for setting the timeframe. Ideally, you want a TRUE goal that includes performance for ten years or longer. I recommend a minimum of five years out; otherwise the goal can tend to be too tactical in focus. By the way, once the goal is reached, a new one will need to be put in place."

TRUE Alignment

Joseph continues teaching. "The TRUE goal sets your most important, future GPS coordinates. You want everyone aligned in the organization and moving towards the same future destination. You want each person to own a part of the TRUE goal. Develop a system to split the TRUE goal into shorter-term objectives and measurable results. The idea is to align employees in an outcome-based and measurable way that ensures traction towards the long term.

"Break the TRUE goal into yearly and quarterly objectives with measurable key outcomes (results). This should be done by division, functional area, department, manager, and employee. Align the TRUE goal to everyone in the organization. Having everyone accountable for performance that is linked to the TRUE goal is a good way to do this.

"While we are on the topic of goals and measures, consider developing a better overall system for measuring your company's performance, specifically, I recommend a strategic dashboard."

Strategic Dashboard

Joseph continues, "It's important to have the right strategic dashboard to track progress. Only include the highest level, most important, and essential measures: not too many. You want to track what matters most to achieving your future success (defined in part by your dream-statement, TRUE goal, and key strategies).

"You need timely and relevant interim measures on Peak Precision Parts' progress towards its future. Good strategic dashboards typically have three to five essential measures. Here are measures to consider on your dashboard." Joseph hands her a list from the Playbook and comments on each measure:

Peak Precision Parts' Strategic Dashboard Considerations

Long-Term (TRUE Goal). Joseph says, "Track the best measure of your TRUE goal—preferably, a measure tied to profitability. Since PPP has high people expenses (578 employees), consider tracking return on invested human capital (people)."

Strategic Customer Value. Joseph comments, "Periodically survey your most important (strategic) customers. Measure how well PPP is delivering unique and relative value (the top and bottom parts of the CURVE). Work with your leadership team and outside research experts (as needed) to identify the best methods and process to measure strategic customer value."

Organizational Health. Joseph comments, "Defining the right problems often gets you halfway to the right solutions. Periodically measuring the health of your organization and its culture helps define people problems. People make or break organizations. If there is dissatisfaction, dysfunction, or some other people related (organizational health) problem, it is holding back success. Diagnose where your company is unhealthy. Involve your human resource folks to come up with the best survey or other approach to measure Peak Precision Parts' organizational health. Measure organizational health every year or two."

<u>Free Cash Flow</u>. Joseph explains, "This represents the amount of actual cash that your company takes in over and above the money it needs to cover all of its operating expenses and new capital expenditures. With the recent changes in your banking situation, a frequent measure of free cash flow (weekly, monthly, quarterly) and how well you are meeting bank covenants will be useful. Even after transitioning out of your short-term financial constraints, you may want to continue to track cash at regular, perhaps longer intervals."

Beautiful Dreams

Joseph presents a challenge to Elizabeth. "You have personally experienced Dr. Martin Luther King's ability to powerfully articulate a dream. There is no better example or role model. You now have knowledge on how to create a dream-statement.

"I challenge you to use this wisdom to create a Peak Precision Parts dream-statement. Do this with your leadership team. Teaching your team the keys to a FATE dream-statement is a good starting place. Creating a specific draft will make it easier to reflect on and refine it.

"After your dream-statement is thoughtfully optimized, define your TRUE long-term goal. Then develop an effective way to measure your progress along your journey with a strategic dashboard and shorter-term objectives and key measures. These steps will give the organization greater clarity and help you lead Peak Precision Parts to greatness."

At 6:15 AM, Elizabeth is awakened by a Paul McCartney song playing on her smart phone alarm: "Ebony and ivory, live together in perfect harmony. Side by side, on my piano keyboard, oh Lord, why don't we?"

Elizabeth contemplates her dream-journey and says to herself, "How appropriate."

She takes Joseph's challenge to heart. Elizabeth educates the Peak Precision Parts' leadership team on how to develop a FATE dream-statement. After extensive discussions, significant mind sweat, and dozens of revisions, the team comes up with the following:

> **Peak Precision Parts' Dream**: *Prolong the joys of life by creating and manufacturing complex, mission-critical medical parts, more rapidly and accurately than anyone thought possible.*

Collectively, the leadership team reviews their new dream-statement against FATE:

Future Dream?
Markus, the Director of HR says, "*'Prolong the joys of life'* answers how the company is going to make a positive difference in the world…it brings into focus a remarkable future dream that is better than the current reality. It is aspirational enough to motivate transformative change."

Align?
Art, the head of PPP sales, says, "The entire dream-statement aligns the organization behind a better future. Our leadership team is totally bought into this dream. It will drive commitment and guide the company in important decisions going forward."

Teach Strategy?
Lisa, the VP of Operations, chimes in, "*'Rapidly and accurately'* and *'creating and manufacturing complex, mission-critical medical parts'* teach how the organization aspires to build and preserve competitive advantage."

Easy to Share?

Steve, the CFO, proclaims, "The old Peak Precision Parts' vision statement that your father developed was 153 words long. With twenty-two words, our new dream-statement is specific, clear, and concise. All words count. It will be easy to communicate and share, internally and externally."

Regarding the long-term (TRUE) goal, the leadership team assesses their individual and collective risk tolerance. Collectively, they average a "7" with a range from "4" to "9." The team goes back and forth on the "explosiveness" and time frame of the goal.

They choose ten years with reasonably aggressive improvements in both return on invested capital (ROIC) and return on invested human capital (ROIHC). Yearly milestones are identified. They agree to revisit their initial TRUE goal choices after they work through their investments (capital and people), strategies, and tactics.

The leadership team defines a strategic dashboard to measure progress. It is based on Joseph's recommendations. The leadership team plans to engage all managers and employees within PPP to develop and own tactical objectives, goals, and measures linked to the dream-statement, TRUE goal, strategic dashboard, annual budgeting, and performance review processes.

The leadership team realizes that they need to articulate clearer values. For the time being, Elizabeth holds on drafting them. Joseph mentioned that he has valuable insights on crafting effective values, and he will share them with her in another dream-journey.

Treasure 1
Define The Dream

Sage Lesson & Background

Dr. Martin Luther King Jr. (1929-1968). King's masterful "I Have a Dream" speech and life accomplishments illustrate the importance and power of defining a dream-statement. A great dream-statement will increase the chances of success of any organization.

King was an American pastor, civil rights activist, and leader. At the time, Martin Luther King was the youngest person to receive the Nobel Peace Prize (1964; he was thirty-five years old). Posthumously, King was awarded the Presidential Medal of Freedom (1977) and the Congressional Gold Medal (2004). In the United States, he is the only non-president to have a national holiday dedicated to his honor. There are over 900 street signs throughout the world named after Martin Luther King.

Key Learnings

❑ Organizations that seek enduring success can benefit from a well-defined **dream-statement**, *a strategic, aspirational, easy-to-grasp description of a more remarkable, better future state of the organization.*

❑ Invest time and effort to define a thoughtful, well-crafted dream-statement. **Use FATE guidelines** (Future dream; Align; Teach strategy; Easy to share) to articulate a clear, focused, and inspiring future beyond just profit.

❑ Your dream-statement is part of the strategic foundation of your company. **Use it as a guiding compass** to align strategies and employees, make decisions, and recruit people who believe in and want to create your future.

❑ Measure what matters. **Develop a TRUE goal** (Tied-to-profit; Risk-aligned; Unmistakable; Explosive) that looks out five or more years, taking care to link the audacity of your goals with your team's risk tolerance and your company's profit implications. Focusing on profit increases the organization's potential to make a positive difference—to be a force for good.

❑ **Develop a Strategic Dashboard** with five or fewer of the most important measures to track interim progress and trends.

❑ **Align** your dream-statement, TRUE goal, strategies, objectives, and tactics throughout your organization so that individuals and teams have clarity, commitment, and accountability in their respective roles.

TREASURE

2

NICHE THE NEW

It's late on a Sunday evening. While dozing off to sleep, Elizabeth hears her grandfather clock strike the bell twelve times. Joseph appears and starts teaching as if he has just left her. "I'd like to introduce you to gravity-shifts. Here are facts and examples that illustrate their importance." Joseph hands Elizabeth a list from the Strategic Playbook:

Gravity-Shifts: Facts & Examples

o <u>Fortune 500</u>: Of the companies that were on the Fortune 500 list in 1955, only 12% remained in 2017.

o <u>Artificial Intelligence</u>: Companies are leveraging shifts towards computerized machines that analyze sophisticated data, automate tasks, problem solve, make decisions, and learn.

o <u>Average Lifespan</u>: The average lifespan in 2018 was 78.8 years. It is projected to extend three months a year. This will create significant niche opportunities within housing, healthcare, and other age-related industries.

o <u>Healthcare</u>: The personal family physician who made home visits with a doctor's bag, shifted to impartial clinics, HMO's, PPO's, and the Affordable Care Act. Concierge health care niches and real time self-diagnostics are evolving the doctor-patient relationship.

o <u>Communication</u>: Smartphone subscriptions are projected to exceed 7 billion by 2023. Most of the world will be able to portably access much of world's knowledge through Wikipedia, DuckDuckGo, Google, Bing, and other websites.

o Personal Transportation: Ford's economical Model T shifted to differentiated GM automobiles, to lower-priced Japanese imports, to electrified, software-based, self-driving vehicles, and ride-sharing.

o Energy: Coal and fossil fuels are shifting to renewables (solar, wind). This is presenting off-the-grid niche solutions that are less tethered to big energy companies.

o E-Commerce & App-Driven Service Transformations: Banking, investing, and in-store merchandising outlets are shifting to e-commerce. Restaurant, hospitality, transportation, and other consumer reservation and appointment habits are shifting to app-driven solutions.

o Artistic Styles: Impressionism shifted to abstract expressionism, to modernism, to pop art, to shock art, to representational realism. More shifts are underway as computer software and 3-D printing offer unique, new ways for artists to express their creativity.

o Music Styles: Big-band (jazz) shifted to rock-and-roll, to disco, hip-hop, rap, and eventually back to classic rock. These shifts create evolving niche opportunities for the music industry.

Gravity-Shifts, Niches & Riches

Elizabeth shifts into learning mode. Joseph continues to teach: "No organization succeeds when it becomes complacent. Everyone needs to *niche the new*—to become good at niche innovation.

"Gravity-shifts create new niche opportunities whether caused by changes in customer preferences, technology, competition, economic cycles, political factors, demographics, or other factors. Gravity-shifts can be either friends or foes.

"To survive, or better yet, thrive, its's a good idea to pay attention to important trends and take advantage of gravity-shifts. Avoid negative shifts. Focus on the right niches to limit competition and build uniqueness that customers value. This is the antidote to commodity (me-too) products and services, which are losing bets.

"Here's a key point: *When pursuing your next niche frontier, it is preferable to have gravity working for you— not against you.*"

Elizabeth responds, "I understand. Please say more."
Joseph continues, "The old saying, '*there are riches in niches,*' often rings true. No one has unlimited resources. There is limited supply of energy, money, people, and other precious resources. To increase the odds of success and gain a better return on your resources, it is wise to *narrow* niche choices. This can be done by differentiated customer offerings that uniquely satisfy needs. You can also niche the new by geography, customer targeting, price, distribution methods, and other choices.

"When selecting niches, concentrate on customer segments that truly appreciate your *unique and superior* differences and that build competitive advantage. Niche the new where you can be first to get it right. Pursue niches where you can build a strong CURVE (Customer Unique and Relative Value Equation). Invest in the top part of the CURVE (what customers uniquely and relatively get) and the bottom part (what customers relatively pay) when creating a platform or stream of strategically linked niche products and services.

"A good way to think about niches, as Michael Porter articulated well, is 'choosing to create your own event...choosing a path different than others...competing to be unique.' Select niches where there are high barriers to being copied. Innovate in niches where you have strengths that competitors can't easily duplicate. Own a niche position where you can uniquely win.

"Compete where the advantages in your chosen niche deliver superior financial performance. Profit helps you attract and reward top employees, suppliers, and customers. It enables you to invest in your future.

"Focus and connect your innovation strategies with tactics. Good strategy is a series of wise, connected choices that reinforce and strengthen tactics."

The Master Spotter (Innovator)

"Now that you have background on gravity-shifts and niches, let's discover how Steve Jobs niched the new. Innovation was in his DNA. He pursued it constantly. It was an essential component of the dream-statement Jobs articulated for Apple:

> *'To build an enduring company where people are motivated to create great products.'*

"To endure, Jobs strongly believed that Apple had to keep developing new products. His mantra successfully countered negative gravity-shifts. This sometimes meant that Apple had to shift into adjacent markets such as music delivery, retail, and cellphones. Jobs played a good balance of offense and defense. He leveraged technology disruptions and found the gravity where overall trends intersected with niche opportunities. As a result, Apple successfully leveraged gravity-shifts."

Something Spotted

Joseph shares why Steve Jobs is a good sage for the Niche The New Treasure. "There is the obvious reason—he was brilliant at it. Here are additional reasons. First, Jobs didn't invent many things outright. But he was a master spotter. He was a master at putting together ideas, art, and technology in unique ways that helped invent the future.

"Ideas are a dime a dozen. Ideas that work are rare. Master spotters are particularly adept at discovering innovations that can work in the marketplace. Successful innovation requires balancing creativity with function. It requires meshing unmet customer needs with the company's unique strengths.

"Jobs spotted important gravity-shifts—both offensively and defensively. He looked at lateral ideas from other niches. Jobs was always searching, connecting, discovering concrete examples of what to do and not do. He looked at Bauhaus furniture, Porsche cars, Cuisinart mixers: anything that could help him visualize a potential new product. Jobs went out into the world and found answers that worked.

"Jobs looked at existing ideas for innovation niches. For example, there were several portable music players on the market before Apple seriously considered introducing their own version, the iPod. None of the competitors had the benefits that Apple brought to the table. Here's a key point: *Seeing opportunities with existing products and uniquely and agilely improving on them can be an effective niche the new approach.*"

Two Heads—Better Than One

Joseph continues, "Another reason Jobs is our innovation sage is because he brought together the right product and design talent. He knew that the customer experience was shaped not only by the product's benefits and features but by the product's aesthetics and interface (including the packaging, advertising, and anything else the customer saw or touched)."

Actions Speak Louder Than Ideas

"Lastly, Jobs made ideas happen. Ideas don't mean a thing until they ring at the cash register (customers are purchasing them). Jobs made innovation look easy—simply spot the right opportunity and have the right talent and resources to make the right ideas happen—before competition."

Simple Apple

Elizabeth and Joseph dream-journey to Cupertino, California. It's a late March evening in 1981. They witness Steve Jobs wearing his iconic Levi's jeans. His long shirt sleeves are rolled up. All 72 inches and 160 pounds of Steve Jobs are completely engaged. He is with James Ferris (Apple Creative Services Director). They are having a dialogue about the Macintosh computer's product design attributes.

Jobs says, "We need to have a classic look that won't go out of style, like the Volkswagen Beetle." After further volleying, they settle on a Porsche as a potential design inspiration for the Macintosh computer.

Through intuitive research, laterally looking at other product categories, and taking a longer-term view, Jobs refined his product and design innovation principles for Apple. He did not want complicated. He did not want slick. He did not want gaudy. Jobs wanted Apple products that were simple, pure, and authentic. In Jobs' words:

> "We will make them bright and pure and honest…we're really shooting for Museum of Modern Art quality. The way we're running the company, the product design, the advertising, it all comes down to this: let's make it simple. Really simple."

Jobs' notion of less is better (simple) also meant that Apple products must be easy-to-use. To quote Jobs, "The main thing in our design is that we have to make things intuitively obvious."

While Jobs did not create the mock-ups for the product designs, he set the principles for the product and design innovations. He obsessed with minute details that made up the overall impression of the products and the company. He had a holistic yet meticulous view. The products, packaging, store designs, what was on the screens, how you assess the products, the advertising…all these elements were linked around his product and design innovation principles.

Front-End Principles

Joseph brings up a useful approach to innovation. "When it comes to innovation, front-end the thinking. Establish and combine the right product (service) and design innovation principles and strategies upfront. This will help maximize differentiated customer value. It will provide superior user experiences. It will reduce rework and get you to your dream quicker.

"Write a succinct one-pager that codifies Peak Performance Parts' medical device product and design innovation principles. Start with version 1.0. Update the document as you refine your thinking. Communicate these principles to everyone entrusted and involved with your innovation efforts."

Not As Easy As 1, 2, 3

Joseph continues, "Let's talk about the iPod, an Apple innovation. Our story starts with Sony's Walkman. Introduced in 1979, the Sony Walkman was a precursor to the iPod. It provided customizable, individual, and portable (on the move) music via cassette tape technology.

"Cassette technology gravitated towards the CD format. Sony's Discman was introduced in 1984. The CD format offered improved sound quality. However, portable CD players had limitations. Before Apple's iPod introduction, the portable music player market had a trifecta of unmet consumer needs. Consumers wanted: 1) large capacity; 2) extended use in a portable device; and 3) ease of use (downloading, accessing music).

"Until 2001, technology and imagination had not yet caught up to satisfy those desires. That shifted when Jon Rubinstein (Apple Senior VP of hardware) visited Japan. He discovered a 1.8-inch by 0.2-inch-thick Toshiba disc drive. It could store a thousand songs. It did not significantly drain a battery. This solved two of the three unmet consumer needs (large song capacity and extended use in a portable device). The third problem still needed to be solved—ease of use."

More Answers

Apple's successful debut of iTunes on January 9, 2001, at Macworld in San Francisco, set the stage for Apple's introduction of a portable music player. One of the main benefits of Apple's iTunes was the ease of organizing and accessing large quantities of music choices.

When creating iTunes, the development team wanted to allow customers the ability to transfer songs from iTunes to the portable MP3 players of the day. So, they integrated Apples' FireWire technology and software with the launch of iTunes.

This proved to be beneficial for the development of Apple's portable music player. Apple's FireWire provided blazing fast downloading speeds—up to thirty times faster than the standard at the time. Onwards to solving the last big problem—a more intuitive, easy to use customer interface for Apple's portable music player device.

Wheel of Fortune

Elizabeth and Joseph dream-journey to the fourth-floor conference room at Apple headquarters in April 2001. Up to that point, Apple was a computer company. It had yet to venture into mass market consumer devices such as portable music players and smartphones.

The few existing portable digital players were poorly designed with respect to loading and accessing music. Capacity was limited. The iPod's product design objectives focused on integrating software and hardware into a device that could satisfy the three unmet consumer needs. It wouldn't hurt if Apple could throw in a bit of cool factor, too.

Meanwhile, back in the conference room, a new product code-named P-68 was on the agenda. Steve Jobs and various members of the P-68 innovation team were looking at prototypes for their new portable music player.

Phil Shiller (Apple Senior VP of Worldwide Product Marketing) shows Jobs several iPod prototypes. Elizabeth and Joseph overhear Phil talk about his idea of how to simply access P-68's song list. He explains to Steve Jobs, "Wouldn't it be great if you could have a wheel?"

"That's It!" Jobs shouts out in a eureka moment. How the customer personally interacted with the iPod was of prime importance to Jobs. The scroll-wheel was the answer for which he was searching.

Apple now had a seamless solution offering a trifecta of differentiated customer offerings in the portable music player market—they were ready to niche the new.

1,000 Songs in My Pocket

Elizabeth and Joseph travel forward six months to October 23, 2001. They are in front row seats in Apple Town Hall, an auditorium on the Cupertino (CA) campus. This is a low-key event compared to typical Apple new product announcements.

Jobs is on stage. He is wearing glasses, a black turtleneck shirt, and his standard Levi's jeans. Everyone is waiting as he introduces P-68. It is now branded the Apple iPod. Jobs says, "To have your whole music library with you at all times is a quantum leap in listening to music...but the coolest thing about iPod is that your entire music library fits in your pocket...I happen to have one right here in my pocket as matter of fact." He reaches into his Levi's jeans front pocket. Jobs pulls out the iPod and shows it to the audience. It is about the size of a deck of cards.

"Here it is, right there...this amazing little device holds a thousand songs, and it goes right into my pocket." Elizabeth and Joseph are close enough to see a minimalist, less-is-better design.

P-68 (Apple iPod)

During Jobs' iPod introduction, there is very little applause. Elizabeth says to Joseph, "The audience does not appreciate what Jobs has just held up in the air."

Later in the day, Elizabeth and Joseph read the Apple iPod press release. It echoes Jobs' comments from earlier in the day. "With iPod, listening to music will never be the same again…Apple has applied its legendary expertise in human interface engineering to make iPod the easiest to use digital device ever. Simply rotate iPod's unique scroll-wheel with your thumb or finger to quickly access your entire music collection by playlists, artists, or songs."

Unlike the early days of Apple computer, the iPod was a team effort. Jobs matured as the innovation leader. He better leveraged and appreciated the talents of his P-68 team. The iPod brought coolness back to the genius of Cupertino. It also brought significant growth. Sales would climb to over 300 million units over the next decade. More important, the iPod was a gateway to Apple's next amazing niche the new opportunity—the iPhone.

Innovation Insights

After their enlightening Steve Jobs' dream-journeys, Joseph shares a list from the Strategic Playbook. It identifies insights into Steve Jobs' innovation successes. Joseph says, "This list can be useful to Peak Precision Parts as you prepare to innovate in the medical devices market." He hands it to her:

Insights Into Innovation Success—Steve Jobs:

o   Had a clear and compelling dream-statement. He created something beyond him. He saw things differently. He had the audacity, vision, and courage to make things happen, no matter what. He sold the dream. He got people to buy into a better Apple future.
o   Set a high pace. He got to the core of issues fast. There

was little wasted time. He had intense focus. He made rapid decisions once he saw the right possibilities.

o Tapped into the right top talent. He believed in and pursued only A+ players. Jobs had zero tolerance for poor talent—in his words, "no bozos."

o Spotted and leveraged positive gravity-shifts. Jobs was great at learning and improving ideas. He found patterns and leveraged them. Jobs saw the relationship between seemingly unconnected ideas and forged them. He made instinctive lateral leaps. To quote Jobs, "What a computer is to me is the most remarkable tool that we have ever come up with. It's the equivalent of a bicycle for our minds." He figured out what customers wanted before they did.

o Kept things simple. He did not get caught in a complexity trap.

o Collaborated early in the innovation process to rapidly identify many options. Jobs quickly culled the list and identified the best prospects. Once the big idea was identified, he went full steam ahead.

o Set the highest standards and front-ended the thinking by identifying and combining product and design innovation principles. He obsessed over detail. Unlike many companies, he integrated designers and product engineers in the innovation process. This improved the customer value impression and experience. It led to a competitive advantage.

o Matured. Early on, Jobs controlled many of the product and design decisions. Later, he gave more autonomy to Apple's new product teams.

o Was acutely aware of negative gravity-shifts—external and internal threats. Jobs proactively took actions to protect Apple's interests (best defense is a good offense).

o Avoided getting into less important businesses. To quote Steve Jobs:

"People think focus means saying yes to the thing you've got to focus on. But that's not what it means at all. It means saying no to the hundred other good ideas that there are. You have to pick carefully. I'm actually as proud of the things we haven't done as the things I have done. Innovation is saying no to 1,000 things."

Innovate or Else

After reviewing the list, Joseph states: "Innovation is not an option. It's a necessity!

"As we have just witnessed from visiting Jobs, if you want to be an enduring company, you must reinvent the organization in synch with gravity-shifts. Hewlett Packard started as an instrument company. It morphed into calculators, computers, and printers. The Rolling Stones started as a blues rock band. They continued to evolve their music. Disney started with a mouse. It evolved into cartoons, movies, TV, theme parks, family entertainment, and international expansion. To succeed long-term, continue to niche the new."

Absolute Advantage

Joseph discusses the importance of relative customer advantages. "Innovation is a relative game. You want your niche the new efforts to be unique as compared to your relevant competitors' innovations.

"To that end, it's essential to find the customer pain-points and unmet or hidden needs that you can uniquely satisfy. The iPod is a good example of focusing on three unmet but important customer needs. Apple was first to get it right in satisfying those needs and was richly rewarded.

"Aim high. Aspire to create products and services with an *absolute advantage*—an ideal state where customers *do not emotionally or rationally consider other choices*. Find advantages that are difficult to copy or are hard for competitors to identify. That is where true innovation treasure can be found. The key to the game is meaningful and relative uniqueness.

"An absolute advantage is very difficult to attain. It's even harder to sustain. Competition does not sit still. However, pursuing an absolute advantage is a way to set a very high bar to create a sustainable competitive advantage and achieve enduring success." Joseph reminds her, "Niche customers have choices. If you can satisfy their emotional and rational needs so well that they don't consider other choices, you will be amazingly successful. Under Steve Jobs, Apple came close to doing this for a fairly long stretch."

3-Keys-Strategy

Elizabeth confesses to Joseph, "Our journey to witness Steve Jobs innovate was fascinating, but I am no Steve Jobs. Nor do we have a Steve Jobs on the Peak Precision Parts' team. How do we go about narrowing our niche choices?"

Joseph replies, "Good innovation reinforces your strategy. Evolve your innovation strategy as you purposely learn. No one has 20/20 foresight. Define a 3-Keys-Strategy for your niche innovations. Refine and build it over time as you learn what works and how to make it more robust. A 3-Keys-Strategy helps you focus. It helps you win.

"There are three key choices that form your 3-Keys-Strategy." Joseph hands Elizabeth a page out of the Playbook that describes and visualizes the 3-Keys-Strategy:

3-Keys-Strategy: 3 Choices

1. Define What Are Your Key **Differentiated Niche Offerings**. Choose what are the most important differentiated niche offerings that you are going to provide that uniquely satisfy customer needs (avoid head-to-head competition—do not offer "me-too" products or services). This helps identify a core group (platform) of niche products or services (current and future) that are meaningfully differentiated and strategically linked.

2. Define Who is Your **Strategic Customer**. Choose who is the most important niche customer you are going to specifically target. Be very selective—say no to non-strategic customers. These are carefully selected crème de la crème target customers. They represent the absolute top prospects. Ideally, they are not the same as your competition.

3. Define Your **Price Segment**. Choose a high or low price segment on which you will focus. It's important to focus on one price segment for your niche. Do not extend into the other price segment with the same brand. If you choose the high price segment, you will need to offer more differentiated value within your niche (top part of the CURVE). If you choose the low price segment, it's important to have a relatively low cost structure to support low price (bottom part of the CURVE).

"Let's review Apple with respect to the three key choices."
Joseph hands Elizabeth the Strategic Playbook
interpretation of Apple's 3-Keys-Strategy:

1. Differentiated Niche Offerings. Elegant, simplified
digital products that provide superior user experiences
(ease-of-use, seamless integration, exceptional purchase,
and follow-up support).

2. Strategic Customer. Middle to upper income consumers
who have discerning tastes for integrated digital products.

3. Price Segment. Apple chooses the high price segment.
They choose to offset a premium price with superior and
differentiated value (what customers uniquely and
relatively get—the top part of the CURVE).

Joseph switches the conversation to Peak Precision Parts.
"Now let's think about Peak Precision Parts' 3-Keys-

Strategy. The good news is that you have already identified strategic niche choices. They are in your dream-statement:

> 'Peak Precision Parts' Dream: *Prolong the joys of life by creating and manufacturing complex, mission-critical medical parts, more rapidly and accurately than anyone thought possible.'*

"Let's discuss the first part of your 3-Keys-Strategy—defining what are your key differentiated niche offerings that uniquely satisfy customer needs."

Elizabeth picks up the ball. "I see that *'more rapidly and accurately'* are key niche offerings that we want to pursue. These are differentiators. These are advantages that we can continue to build. We want to be involved in prototyping: the early stages of design. We have engineers who are exceptional at this. This is a reason we added *'creating'* to our dream-statement." Joseph replies, "Bravo. This is a good start.

"*'Creating and manufacturing complex, mission-critical parts'* narrows your target. Clearly, you want to target medical device companies who desire outsourced solutions." Elizabeth answers, "Yes, we want companies that outsource. More importantly, we want to target companies that require complex, mission-critical parts (CMCP)." Joseph responds, "Good...I assume you want to focus on profitable and large customers too." Elizabeth concurs.

Joseph continues, "Based on this conversation, you have a start in answering the second part of your 3-Keys-Strategy—defining who is your strategic customer. Your strategic customers are the most important. I suggest you clearly define the minimum target amount of business that is acceptable and what 'profitable' means. We will revisit these points and further refine your strategic customer definition in another dream-journey.

"That leaves price. Any idea as to what price segment you want to compete — where you can profitably win?" Elizabeth says, "We need to migrate back to the high price segment. We have lost ground because of a lack of focus...chasing 'me-too' exceptions that were lower priced and had poor margins (commodities). We did this to cover overhead. Sadly, the company has evolved to a mindset that any revenue is good revenue. It's clear to me that low-price does not make sense for us."

Elizabeth and Joseph place the preliminary PPP 3-Keys-Strategic choices within the triangle:

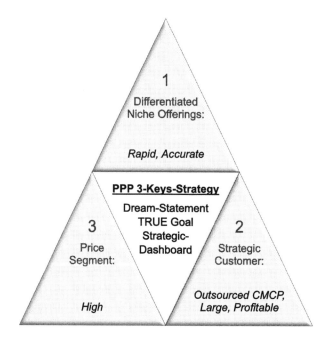

Joseph sums up their discussion on the 3-Keys-Strategy. "Clarity in the 3-Keys-Strategy helps the company focus on the most important product and service strategies (what to do and not do). It gives clear line of sight of where to keep building uniqueness and advantage relative to customers' other choices. It provides the arena (niche) where your organization plays, competes, and improves.

"Your 3-Keys-Strategy needs to be further optimized. This will take time. Improving the 3-Keys-Strategy and related products and services is an ongoing effort. As reference, the iPod was continually improved to stay in front of evolving technology and competition. Excluding the Mini, Nano, Shuffle, and Touch, between October 23, 2001 and September 9, 2009, there were seven generations of the iPod."

Important No's

Joseph continues teaching. "A successful 3-Keys-Strategy requires that you make important choices as to how you will play and win your game. It requires that you say no to everything that does not support your strategy.

"Once you decide what is most important, it will be easier to weed out the less important. The hard part will be saying no to good opportunities that are not the absolute best. That is where leadership comes in to play. Saying no to everything but the most important separates good strategy from great strategy."

Visual Recap

Joseph provides a recap. "Good strategic choices strengthen your CURVE. They provide the right strategic direction. They lead to higher, more sustained profitability and a stronger competitive advantage. Here is a visual depiction of important concepts we have discussed." Joseph hands Elizabeth an illustration comparing a weak and strong CURVE and defining the right strategic direction from the Playbook:

Customer Unique and Relative Value Equation (CURVE)

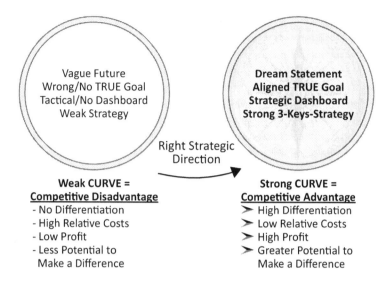

Vague Future
Wrong/No TRUE Goal
Tactical/No Dashboard
Weak Strategy

Dream Statement
Aligned TRUE Goal
Strategic Dashboard
Strong 3-Keys-Strategy

Right Strategic
Direction

Weak CURVE =
Competitive Disadvantage
- No Differentiation
- High Relative Costs
- Low Profit
- Less Potential to
  Make a Difference

Strong CURVE =
Competitive Advantage
➤ High Differentiation
➤ Low Relative Costs
➤ High Profit
➤ Greater Potential to
  Make a Difference

The Question

Joseph continues, "Now that you have a good start on a 3-Keys-Strategy, how is Peak Precision Parts going to niche the new?"

Elizabeth responds, "I agree that innovation is essential to our long-term success. I see three immediate steps. First is to bring the team up to speed on what I've learned. The Strategic Playbook items you've provided me with will make it easier to transfer the knowledge.

"Second, we need to better understand the medical device market from the customer and competitor perspectives. This will help us refine our 3-Keys-Strategy and related competitive advantages.

"The third step is to find the right innovation talent. It will not be easy. This will keep me up at night."

One More Thing

Elizabeth and Joseph dream-journey to her home. They discuss the fact that innovation is not a strong suit for many organizations. Elizabeth refers to PPP's Competitive Comparison Questions survey results. "Our second lowest score was for the question about innovation abilities. Do you have any ideas to help find the right innovation talent?"

Joseph replies, "Yes. Use CliftonStrengths (Strength-Finders) to identify candidates with right brain strengths such as Ideation, Strategic, Futuristic. These will help with the 'spotter' side of innovation. Look for left brain strengths such as Activator, Achiever, and Arranger. These will help with the implementation side of innovation.

"Here is 'one more thing.'" He hands Elizabeth a document from the Strategic Playbook. It is a list of innovation leader expectations and success characteristics (behaviors). He comments, "While I recommend that a collaborative, balanced, and multi-functional innovation team develops your new niche products, I strongly recommend that you have one medical device innovation leader. This will give you a start on identifying and recruiting your Steve Jobs. Edit, add to, and improve the expectations and success characteristics, as you see fit."

Peak Precision Parts' Innovation Leader Expectations & Success Characteristics

Overall, this position is essential to creating a better future for Peak Precision Parts (PPP). The innovation leader will be a major contributor in building the medical device parts business. They will take the leading role in new product creation and strategic niche optimization. Below are the expectations and success characteristics for this role:

- o Actively searches for and spots the right niche innovation opportunities. Takes the initiative to identify and focus attention on those few innovations which can have a major impact on prolonging the joys of patients' lives. Leads the Innovation Team to create complex, mission-critical medical parts, more rapidly and accurately than anyone thought possible. Identifies strategic niche areas to remain and be strengthened and ones to avoid.
- o Intentionally increases competitive advantage. Ensures that changes are not reactive responses but are well thought out strategic choices that build sustainable product and service platforms.
- o Ensures all innovations are aligned with PPP's dream-statement, 3-Keys-Strategy, and long-term goals. Thinks through the right product and design principles and strategies—before expensive prototyping.
- o Leads the Innovation Team to innovate, fail, learn, and scale more quickly than competition. Sets the standard for and establishes a high pace of profitable growth. Determines agile ways to improve PPP's prototyping and product development speed while ensuring accuracy. Has a strong sense of urgency to realize short and long-term objectives and key outcomes.
- o Thinks multi-dimensionally, strategically, and creatively about the medical device business. Plans for the long term. Identifies the right gravity-shifts (positive and negative trends). Objectively analyzes customer research, current, and future competitive positions, and other relevant information. Quickly assimilates this information along with good judgment and intuition.

o Truly understands customers' hearts and minds. Asks the right questions and listens well. Uses these skills to accurately understand customer experiences, insights, pain-points, hidden and unmet needs, aspirations, and competitive positions. Develops a hierarchy of strategic customer niche offerings that uniquely satisfy customer needs. Uses this to improve PPP's customer unique and relative value equation (CURVE).

o Sets the highest standards for excellence. Does this in collaboration with the Peak Precision Parts' Innovation Team.

o Builds and maintains productive working relationships with the Innovation Team and people in other departments, including those who may have different points of view and who are not direct reports.

o Consistently lives PPP's values.

o Is accountable for bringing new products to market on time and within budget.

After reviewing the document, Elizabeth thanks Joseph and makes an interesting observation. "Your Innovation Leader Expectations & Success Characteristics leverage all the niche the new principles we have explored on this dream-journey." Joseph smiles.

Treasure 2
Niche The New

Sage Lesson & Background

Steve Jobs (1955-2011). Jobs teaches the necessity of having the right innovation leadership to identify (spot), develop, and bring to market successful niche products and services that build competitive advantage. Jobs proves that you do not have to come up with the idea. It's more about spotting the right opportunities and successfully leading the organization to niche the new. He reminds us that companies and organizations must innovate. Otherwise, you can suffer the consequences that competition will make you obsolete.

Jobs was an American entrepreneur, business executive, and cofounder of Apple. He led the introduction of innovations that transformed seven industries (personal computers, animated movies, music, phones, tablet computing, digital publishing, and retail stores). Jobs helped create a company that became the first to reach $1 trillion in stock market valuation (source: August 2, 2018, stock market data).

Key Learnings

❑ Refining niches and improving innovation abilities (niche the new) are essential for long-term success.

❑ **Pay attention to Gravity-shifts**, fundamental trends, changes, and disruptions in customer preferences, technology, competition, political factors, economic cycles, demographics, and other factors. **Find innovation intersections** where gravity-shifts work for you (not against you).

❑ Narrow the playing field—say no to less important niche innovation opportunities. Select niches where you can build an enduring competitive advantage. Innovate in niches where you have strengths that competitors can't easily duplicate. **Own a niche position where you can uniquely win**.

❑ Successful companies choose, focus on, and refine a **3-Keys-Strategy**. They: 1) define their differentiated niche offerings that they are going to provide that uniquely satisfy customer needs; 2) decide who is their strategic customer (crème de la crème); and 3) choose and remain in either a high or low-price segment.

❑ **Combine product and design** innovation principles to provide unique, seamless, and superior customer experiences.

❑ When niching the new, **strive for an absolute advantage**, an ideal state where customers do not emotionally or rationally consider other choices.

❑ Successful innovation requires **the right innovation talent**. For maximum success identify one innovation leader who spots the right innovation opportunities, leads the innovation team, and is accountable for ongoing niche the new successes.

TREASURE

3

TAP THE TOP TALENT

Joseph and Elizabeth are in a capacity-filled sports arena. They are sitting courtside behind the visiting team's bench. Elizabeth immediately notices the length of the shorts, tube socks, and white shoes of the players. To overcome the excitement among the fans, Elizabeth speaks loudly as she asks Joseph a basic question, "Where are we?"

Joseph replies, "The visiting team in front of us is undefeated this season (13-0). It has kept alive an impressive forty-seven game winning streak. The home team on the other side is also undefeated. They have a 16-0 season record. Two of the game's top coaches, are about to match wits in this: *The Game of the Century.*

"We have dream journeyed back in time to 1968. We are in the Houston Astrodome with over 52,000 fans. Millions are also watching at home. This is the first regular season NCAA basketball game ever televised on national TV."

Joseph explains to Elizabeth, "This will be a clash of top talent. The UCLA Bruins team is filled with 'A' players including future Hall-of-Famer Lew Alcindor (Kareem Abdul-Jabbar). The Houston Cougars have Elvin Hayes, another future Hall-of-Famer."

The buzzer sounds. Joseph stops his commentary. The teams vie for position as the referee jumps the ball to start the game. Houston plays an aggressive paced, above the rim game. Elvin Hayes scores a game high 39 points.

He pulls down 15 rebounds and leads Houston to an upset. UCLA loses in the final seconds, 71- 69.

After the game, there is no blame, excuse, or criticism of the Houston Cougars. Wooden is humble in defeat—just as he is modest in victory. He reminds the players: "We have to start over. Losing is only temporary and not all-encompassing. You must simply study it, learn from it, and try hard not to lose the same way again." So, the Bruins went back to LA and did what they do best—they prepared.

A Pyramid is Found in LA

Elizabeth and Joseph dream-journey ahead four days. They are at UCLA's newly constructed Pauley Pavilion basketball arena. It is early on a Wednesday morning (January 24, 1968). As they enter the Pavilion, there is a lingering smell of body odor from hard workouts.

They observe Coach John Wooden in his office. On the wall, they see his Pyramid of Success. It is prominently displayed on a bulletin board along with team photos. Wooden is discussing the Pyramid of Success with a newspaper reporter.

The Pyramid of Success has fifteen building blocks with carefully chosen and optimized Wooden words and phrases. Wooden states, "The position of each block and the specific order of the tiers of blocks in the pyramid have importance."

Elizabeth and Joseph overhear Wooden discuss the talent of his team with the reporter. Wooden points to and describes one of the blocks titled, "Skill." It is in the center of his Pyramid of Success. Wooden says, "I'd rather have a lot of talent and a little experience than a lot of experience and little talent." Wooden continues, "You need to know what you are doing and be able to do it quickly and properly.

Skill means being able to execute all of your job, not just part of it."

Elizabeth notices that the Pyramid's blocks build and point upwards. At the apex is Wooden's written definition of success:

> "Success is peace of mind that is a direct result of self-satisfaction in knowing you did your best to become the best you are capable of becoming."

Preparing to Succeed

After the reporter leaves, Elizabeth and Joseph observe Coach Wooden and his assistant coaches preparing for the day's practice. Wooden has kept detailed accounts of every practice. This information helps them analyze how to conduct the optimal practice for the team and individual players.

Everything is planned. The planning places effort in the practice where it is needed most. Every activity is detailed on three-by-five index cards. For example, at 3:17 PM they will need two basketballs at midcourt for the three players against two drill. The coaches have worked through dozens of drill variations, all with exacting timing and details for today's practice. This goes on for several hours. All told, Wooden and his assistants invest as much time planning the day's practice as they will spend conducting it.

Joseph shares a favorite quote with Elizabeth that Wooden borrowed from Benjamin Franklin:

> "Failing to prepare is preparing to fail."

Later in the day, Elizabeth and Joseph return to the UCLA gym. It is 2:30 PM. Wooden is a stickler for time management. There are no slackers. Everyone is present. The practice is in full swing.

Unlike at the game, Wooden is not wearing a tie. He is working, leading, teaching. Everyone is active, moving, working. Joseph and Elizabeth hear Coach Wooden's enthusiastic commands: "Move! Move! Move!" They overhear Wooden working with a player. "Rebounding is positioning. Being quicker to get into position is worth more than strength."

Squeaking sounds from busy sneakers fill the court. Coach has set a very high tempo. He is preparing them to play under pressure and to play to their potential in a game. He is teaching them to be the best version of themselves.

Practice ends promptly at 4:30 PM. At the conclusion, Coach says to the team, "You have a responsibility for the attainment and maintainment (sic) of all the little details that we did in practice today. Your responsibility begins now. So please practice moderation in what you do before the next practice." Afterwards, Coach writes down thorough notes to be reviewed and analyzed later.

As Joseph and Elizabeth are leaving, they run into Coach. Elizabeth approaches Wooden. "I am amazed at your attention to detail." Coach Wooden responds, "Thank you. These seemingly trivial matters, taken together and added to many, many other so-called trivial matters, build into something very big—namely, success. You will find that success and attention to details, the smallest details, usually go hand in hand, in basketball and elsewhere in life."

Elizabeth asks a question. "Would you mind sharing where you got the inspiration to coach a practice like that?" Without hesitation, Coach Wooden responds. "I had a card that was given to me by my father, Joshua, when I graduated from grade school. It had seven things on it. All he asked of me was to try and live up to the seven things. Number three on that list were the words, 'make each day your masterpiece.' When I teach basketball, I urge my players to try their hardest to improve on this very day, to make this practice a masterpiece."

Practice Impressions & Lessons

After thanking Coach Wooden, Joseph and Elizabeth discuss what they observed in the UCLA Bruins' practice today. "How many organizations do you know have thought about talent as comprehensively and thoroughly as Coach Wooden?" Elizabeth says that she is not aware of any. Joseph then asks Elizabeth, "What about Peak Precision Parts? Do you have effective processes to recruit, train, and retain the right top talent (or said another way, to tap the top talent)?" She responds, "No, we have to improve."

Joseph summarizes, "Coach Wooden is the role model on how to bring the best out of talent by paying attention to the right details in recruiting, coaching, and retention."

Big Rebound

Joseph and Elizabeth dream-journey to the NCAA Men's Semi-Finals on Friday, March 22, 1968. They are behind the home-team bench in the Los Angeles Memorial Sports Arena.

The UCLA Bruins use a diamond-plus-one defense to clamp down on Hayes. This helps take away Houston's talent advantage. It limits Hayes to only ten points (versus thirty-nine in the previous Game of the Century loss). Thorough and rigorous preparation combined with top talent pays off. UCLA wins 109 to 69. According to UCLA's Lynn Shackelford, "That was the best game we played in my four years—the closest we came to our potential."

Five Steps To Top Talent

Elizabeth and Joseph dream-journey to her home in Indiana. Joseph says, "The greatest pain-points managers experience are often related to poor performers, terminations, and the hidden costs of not paying enough attention to recruiting, coaching, and retaining the right top talent. Having great people plans and simple yet effective processes can significantly contribute to achieving competitive advantage and long-term success."

They get into a discussion of how hard it is to recruit the right talent. Joseph refers to PPP's Competitive Comparison Questions survey results. "The question, 'How well does PPP identify, attract, hire, and retain the right top talent,' scored the third lowest."

Elizabeth agrees with the low survey result. She asks Joseph, "Do you have tips on how to improve the odds of attracting and hiring the right talent?" He replies, "Many companies and organizations struggle with the hiring process. I have Five Steps To Top Talent. Most of this is basic, some of it is not. It addresses common pitfalls organizations suffer from and deficiencies lacking in hiring practices and processes. Is it OK to review?" Elizabeth responds, "Yes."

Joseph hands Elizabeth a diagram from the Playbook:

Five Steps To Top Talent

1. Front-End The Right Talent Definition
2. Establish A Magnetic, Targeted Network
3. Optimize Assessment Tools & Techniques
4. Use A Top-Notch Interview Panel
5. Thoroughly Validate Talent

Joseph continues, "These Five Steps increase the odds of tapping the right top talent. As a result, you will have more effective, productive employees. You will reduce turnover, frustration, and stress. You will lessen the hidden costs of the wrong hires."

1. **<u>Front-End The Right Talent Definition</u>**. Joseph explains that a root cause of bad hiring decisions is that roles are not well defined. "There can be different perceived ideas as to what is the definition of the right top talent by the various people recruiting candidates. Ensure everyone is on the same page. Think through what the right requirements and expectations for the position are. Front-end the thinking and create a written, clear, and accurate role description. This will improve your odds of a successful hire." Joseph shares and discusses the right talent definition components from the Playbook:

Overview

A well written Overview helps attract and pre-qualify the right candidates to the company. It's the hook that tells and sells why top talent should consider your opportunity over others. The Overview briefly describes the company. It explains how the role fits with the company's dream-statement and 3-Keys-Strategy. It describes how the position can make a difference (adds value to customers, the organization, and society).

Performance Metrics That Matter

Measure performance that matters most to the position and the organization. Doing this requires thinking through what the right performance goals and key measures for the role are. For example, a sales position might have goals that answer the following questions (goal examples are in parenthesis):

o   How much new gross profit will you realize from strategic customers and by when (greater than $1,000,000 gross profit within 18 months)?
o   What is your successful strategic customer retention rate (100% for the next twelve months)?
o   What is your successful quotation to close rate (greater than 70% average for the next 12 months)?
o   How many influential people will you have meaningful contact with at potential new strategic customers (greater than 20 per quarter for each strategic customer target)?

Only include the most important three to five goals for each role. Prioritize them. Ensure they are clear, specific, measurable, and timebound, not vague. Link at least one to the long-term (TRUE) goal. Use the specific performance goals to help you evaluate and determine if candidates can deliver on them if hired.

Joseph comments, "During the interview, it's important to determine if candidates can perform at a level consistent with the role's performance expectations. Using the Playbook's sales position to illustrate my point, determine if there is enough evidence—is it believable that the candidate can generate $1 million or more gross profit within eighteen months. *This will help you focus on what matters in the interview."*

Key Expectations & Success Characteristics

The next thing to be defined upfront are descriptions of the expectations, behaviors, and characteristics of success for the specific role. Joseph comments, "A useful example (Peak Precision Parts' Innovation Leader) was shared with you during Treasure 2 (Niche The New)." These descriptions are a good source to identify behavior-based interview questions.

Cultural Compatibility

Regarding cultural compatibility, Joseph recommends taking a lesson from Coach Wooden: "Character was so important to Wooden that he would travel to the childhood homes of his top basketball prospects. He learned about the player's personal character from what kind of home in which the player was raised. According to Lew Alcindor (Kareem Abdul-Jabbar), Wooden was the only coach his parents invited up to their apartment, and this made a difference. In Kareem's words: 'There were a lot of reasons for me to pick UCLA. But in the end the only one that really mattered was John Wooden.'"

Joseph continues, "In business, identifying upfront that there is good cultural compatibility is important. Screen for candidates who possess the values of your company. Use behavioral-based interview questions that help uncover if the candidates have PPP's values within their DNA. This is an important step to help retain top candidates long-term. To quote Coach Wooden:

> 'Character creates longevity. I believe ability can get you to the top, but it takes character to keep you there.'"

2. **Establish A Magnetic, Targeted Network**. Elizabeth confesses to Joseph, "We struggle with the challenge of finding enough prospects." Joseph suggests, "Pull talent to your organization versus having to fight and find it. Invest in targeted marketing. It is easier when the best prospects come knocking on your door.

"Let the positive magnetic power of Peak Precision Parts' strengths work for you. Paint the picture of what is unique and better about your organization than other companies.

"The ultimate way to create a strong magnetic pull is to have a successful business, healthy culture, great environment, and to treat employees with fairness and respect.

"Credible testimonials from outside resources can help. Getting on lists of best places to work is effective. Positive statements from existing employees can add to the magnetic pull.

"Peak Precision Parts' website is one of the first things top talent will look at. How well does PPP's website work as a magnet to recruit talent? Design the website, in part, to create an accurate and positive impression of what it is like to work at PPP…have PPP well positioned on LinkedIn and other job-centric websites…check Glassdoor and other job review websites so that you know what is being said about your company.

"A magnetic, targeted network is all about effective target marketing. Use benefit focused messaging that attracts and positions why your company is a better choice for target prospects. Identify targeted media that improve the odds of reaching the best prospects. Leverage unique channels that can increase the number of qualified candidates. Here is a McDonald's in-

restaurant tray liner example that does all of that."
Joseph hands Elizabeth the Playbook example:

McDonald's Tray Liner Talent Magnet Message

Discover all the best parts of working here.
- ✓ **Choose your hours**. No really. Just tell us the hours you are free (and the hours you aren't). We'll work around your needs.
- ✓ **Pursue Higher education**. From high school completion to college tuition assistance, we can help you reach your dreams.
- ✓ **Build your skills**. Wherever you are right now, come here to build the job skills, people skills, and life skills that can take you further.
- ✓ **Delight our guests**. Our team gets to share delicious food, fun moments, and big smiles all day long. Come make happy happen!
- ✓ **Be you**. Around here, you can be who you are, become even more, and move towards your dreams—with a great team to back you up.

McDonald's works for me. Committed to being America's best first job. © 2017 McDonald's.

"This message speaks the WIIFM language (What's In It For Me). It's all about the target customer. It gives McDonald's an advantage over competition in attracting talent. Develop your own unique and proprietary magnets to attract your talent targets."

Joseph recommends that PPP identify target trade schools, universities, companies, and industries that are good sources of qualified talent. "Keep evaluating and refining approaches to reach and pull the best talent.

"After each hire, ask 'what did we learn…is there anything that can improve our talent magnet and refine our targeted network?'"

3. **<u>Optimize Assessment Tools & Techniques</u>**. Elizabeth asks Joseph, "In your opinion, how many candidates are a good target?" He suggests, "As a rule of thumb, twenty. However, it depends on the position and supply. Start broadly. Narrow as you qualify candidates. A funnel approach is essential to increase the numbers and ultimate quality. Sometimes it's difficult to find one, much less twenty. However, your odds of success significantly increase if you have more choices of qualified candidates.

    "After screening resumes, conduct initial email, phone, or video screening interviews. Add more screening effort and scrutiny as the candidates continue to look promising. Keep optimizing screening processes on a return on effort basis."

    Elizabeth says, "We used various screening tools in my past life in hospital administration. What are your thoughts on them?" Joseph replies, "Screening tools can be useful. There are tools to identify candidates' top strengths, reasoning and problem solving abilities, attitudes and personalities, work processes, and other important attributes. Another screening option is to do a work trial period or use work sample and simulations (linked to specific job skills) to see how potential employees perform in action.

    "Regardless what you use, learn the limitations of each screening tool. Many organizations rely too much on them. They overweigh their importance. You need to validate talent screening tools with actual experience. Narrow to the best tools based on experience and results."

4. **<u>Use A Top-Notch Interview Panel</u>**. They turn their attention to the actual interview process. Joseph says, "Another root cause of bad hires can be traced to poor interviewers. Problems occur when organizations do not have a top-notch interview panel. The good news is that good interviewing techniques can be learned."

Elizabeth asks, "Who do you recommend including on the interview panel?" Joseph replies, "The panel must only have the best interviewers on it. You want an interview panel filled with people like Coach Wooden—people who know what they are looking for, are good listeners (do not talk too much), who can properly, objectively, thoroughly, and consistently assess the right top talent. They must have high standards and represent your company well."

Yes or No?

Elizabeth asks about interviewer collaboration. He replies, "Have each member of the interview panel independently evaluate each candidate and independently answer this question: *'Would I hire this person to work for me or not?'* A simple yes or no are the only two choices. This approach keeps standards high."

Best Behaviors

Elizabeth asks, "What are your thoughts on behavior-based interviewing?" Joseph replies, "A good indicator of future performance is past performance. Behavior-based interviewing is an effective approach so long as the interviewers are properly trained and competent interviewers.

"Good behavior-based interviewers use focused and penetrating questions that uncover truth about past performance. They do this better than general 'tell me about your life' questions. The specific behavior-based ('tell me about a time when you...') questions come from the key performance metrics, expectations, success characteristics, and values for the role."

Unique Methods

Elizabeth asks, "Are there special questions you recommend asking?" Joseph responds, "We built a competitive advantage in a company I led by hiring creative problem solvers in every position. We devised the 'lightbulb question' to screen for this talent.

"The lightbulb question was the last one asked of every candidate. We would place a light bulb on the table and set up the situation...'No right or wrong answers...looking for as many approaches as they could think of...please share any ideas that come to mind.' We would then ask; *'how many cubic inches of volume are contained within this light bulb?'*

"We would guide, and prompt follow up questions depending on responses. We learned about the candidate's creative problem-solving skills based on the breadth and depth (quality) of their answers...did they ask clarifying questions, such as *'what problem were we trying to solve...why were we trying to solve it...how does it affect customers?'* We also learned how well candidates could think on their feet. When interacting with customers, sometimes you must quickly think and solve problems on the spot.

"The lightbulb question is shared to illustrate that you can create unique questions and methods to help you assess what is strategically important to Peak Precision Parts. Doing this right can give you an advantage."

5. **Thoroughly Validate Talent**. The last point Joseph covers is the importance of thoroughly validating that the final candidates are what they represent. "Use legal and ethical methods to validate academic credentials, military service, employment history, criminal records, and other relevant areas. It is better to find the truth before hiring someone that misrepresents themselves. You want to flush out candidates that may have issues that can affect job performance."

Elizabeth asks, "What about reference checking? I know from past recruiting efforts at the hospital that liability concerns prevent most human resource departments from sharing anything but name, rank, and serial number." Joseph agrees. He still recommends asking candidates for references. "If you uncover something important for just one out of ten actual hires, that is time well spent. Thoroughly validating talent upfront can save heartache and frustration for the company and the candidate."

Identify and Nurture Stars

Elizabeth thanks Joseph. She asks, "Now that you have reviewed a good process to find and hire the right top talent, do you have ideas on how to retain them? Competitors and other companies are constantly trying to steal our talent. How do we keep top talent on our team?"

Joseph responds, "Start by determining what talent is critical to building the CURVE—where to invest in strategic bench strength. Next, identify existing top talent that has the most future potential—the Stars. These are the agile up-and-comers who drive the value creation in the organization. They consistently perform at the highest levels and have the right stuff for future management and leadership positions. They tend to perform without heavy coaching—they don't need a detailed map. They directly strengthen the CURVE by creating unique customer value and significantly reducing operating costs.

"Many Stars leave because another organization pays more attention to them. Another reason for regrettable Star turnover is because sometimes good people are managed by bad coaches. These and other contributors to Star turnover can be minimized if you develop a system to identify and take care of your Stars. Keep it simple. At least once a year, have all employees assessed. The timing of this assessment does not have to be linked to the performance review process."

Invest in the Best

Joseph continues, "Pay attention to and invest in your Stars. Have them managed by your best coaches. Put them on the best opportunities that leverage their strengths. Provide accelerated training programs. Expose them to programs such as intentional leadership.

"Consistently communicate with all Stars. Set up frequent and periodic meetings to ensure everything is going well. Recognize Stars through positive engagement. Identify and flush out career obstacles or other issues that may interfere with their development. Address issues, as appropriate. Reward Stars and pay them appropriately. This should be easy since by definition, they are top performers.

"A proactive approach to recognizing, nurturing, and retaining Stars will, over time, provide you with a competitive advantage over companies that do a poor job of paying attention to and cultivating their top talent."

Five Steps To Successful Succession

Elizabeth asks Joseph for his recommendations on improving succession planning. "As you know, my father did not have a good succession plan. What do you advise we do to improve?" Joseph replies, "Many organizations do not have an adequate succession process. This can cause major headaches when a key player retires or gets hit by the proverbial bus. Likewise, it can hinder growth if there is inadequate backup talent (bench strength) for key positions. Net, intentional succession is important to future success.

"Take a cue from Coach Wooden. Use a good process, develop a ritual, and stick with it. That's all there is to it. Consistency is paramount. Let me take you through a simple, effective, proven process to get control over succession. For large organizations, the process can be cascaded up and down. It can be implemented by division, team, or function.

"The Five Steps to Successful Succession requires discipline and thoroughness. Think and act like Wooden. Let's work through the steps using your organizational chart." Joseph hands Elizabeth a Playbook diagram that provides an overview of the process:

Five Steps To Successful Succession

1. **Identify Expected Exits & New Positions**. Joseph discusses the diagram. "For the first step, identify all expected exits of existing key positions needed to achieve the long-term (TRUE) goal. Discuss with key employees what their plans are for retirement. You may uncover surprises that you did not expect. It is better to know and plan accordingly.

   "Identify key new positions needed to pursue the dream-statement, 3-Keys-Strategy, and achieve the TRUE goal. As we discussed in Treasure 2 (Niche The New), an Innovation Leader is an essential new PPP hire.

   "What are the expected exits of the key roles to achieve your TRUE goal?" Elizabeth responds, "There are three key positions that I know will retire. And there is the Innovation Leader." Joseph asks, "Can you write their information down please?" Elizabeth does so.

   After Elizabeth provides the information, they create a partial organization chart. Joseph then suggests, "Let's identify key expected exits and new positions with black boxes (versus gray). This helps us see key succession outages. To that end, for a partial PPP org chart, the four positions you identified are depicted in black (VP Operations, VP Sales, Director of Engineering, and the Innovation Leader). Is that correct?" Elizabeth responds, "Yes."

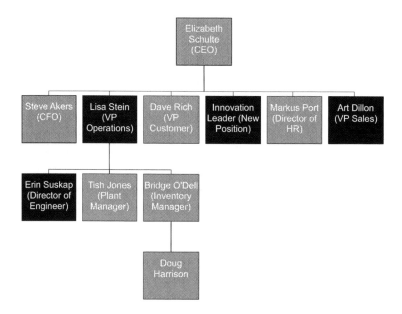

2. **Identify Best Current Options**. "The second step is to identify the best replacement choices for every management and leadership role in the company. Some or many of the names may be unqualified for the position. Regardless, have the best current backup option noted for all positions. Place the name of the best option under every management and leadership position." Elizabeth and Joseph add the best current backup options to the partial PPP organization chart:

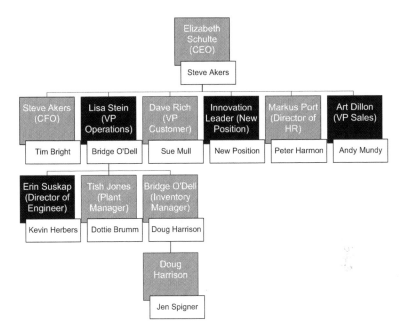

3. **Identify Stars & Timeframes**. "For the third step, we revisit our Star discussion. This is where you find your best internal candidates for future promotions. Stars play a critical role in successful succession plans. They are your strategic bench strength. Taking a company-wide inventory of your Stars and building strength in strategic areas will put you in the driver's seat.

"Let's place a star symbol underneath each Star on our Peak Precision Parts' organization chart. This indicates that the person is a candidate for promotion to that position.

"Next, let's estimate the approximate time frame that each position is expected to retire. If the timeframe is ten years or greater, let's note that. If the timeframe is unknown, let's note that too." Joseph and Elizabeth update the partial PPP organization chart by adding a star symbol where appropriate and the estimated retirement timeframes for all known positions:

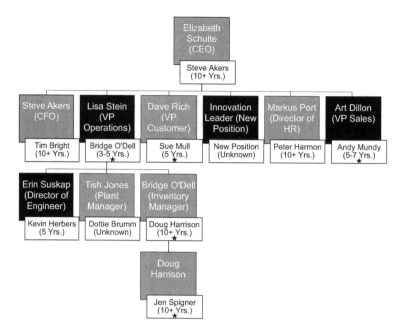

4. **Create a Gap List**. "The next step builds off the first three. This is where you identify the succession gaps that need to be closed. Create a list of all gaps identified from the first three steps. If there is a position that will move up, then that will need a replacement, too. For example, when the VP of Operations retires within five years, you indicated that Bridge O'Dell (Star), is the likely replacement. Her position will need to be added to the gap list. Note, where there is not an acceptable backup, include this in the gap list as well."

Elizabeth asks how far in the future the list should consider. Joseph responds, "Five years is a minimum timeframe for your gap list. Ideally, use a time frame that is consistent with your TRUE goal. In PPP's case, that is ten years."

5. **Define a Prioritized Plan**. Joseph concludes with step five. "Take your gap list and sort succession positions into three priorities (high, medium, and low). High priorities are more critical and vulnerable positions. Pursue closing gaps in priority order. Define and assign accountabilities to close the gaps (who is going to do what and by when). Periodically make succession and accountabilities an agenda topic during leadership team meetings.

   "Thoroughly review succession at least annually. Link it to strategic planning and board meetings. In addition, unexpected key departures will result in changes to the succession plan. When that occurs, reprioritize, as appropriate."

Elizabeth and Joseph work through the gap list. They identify and place succession positions in the appropriate priority categories (high, medium, and low). They make notes alongside each of the respective positions:

High Priorities

A. Innovation Leader—The essential role to lead and develop innovations necessary for strategic and profitable growth (build the CURVE, 3-Keys Strategy, and achieve the TRUE goal). It has high potential to create a lot of unique value. That is why it is listed as the top priority. The position will need to be filled from the outside. Note: look for a Star (potential future President).

B. CEO—Even though Elizabeth plans to be around for a while (she is forty two), no one is ready to take the helm if something unfortunate happens to her. Elizabeth believes the Innovation Leader, or Bridge O'Dell and Andy Mundy (Stars) with five to ten years of additional experience and development can be considerations.

C. VP Operations—Planned retirement within three to five years. This is a critical position for executing on promises and efficiently leveraging resources and costs. Approximately sixty percent of the 578 PPP employees report up to this position. There is a Star in the wings (Bridge O'Dell). She can be promoted to VP of Operations.

Medium Priorities

A. VP Sales—The head of sales is an essential position for future success. A lot of value can be created by this role. PPP has a Star, Andy Mundy, in development. Succession timing works reasonably well for Art Dillon's anticipated retirement in five to seven years.
B. CFO—The CFO role is important to PPP, especially with its tenuous financial position with the bank. The Controller is not strategic enough for the CFO role. If PPP has to hire a new CFO within the next ten years, it will likely recruit from the outside.
C. Director of HR—There is no planned exit within ten years. PPP does not have a Star in place. It will recruit the position from the outside, if needed.

Low Priorities (or Unknown)

A. VP Customer Care—Retirement for this position is ten plus years away. There is a Star in the wings (Sue Mull). With five or more years of additional development, there will likely be a smooth transition for the VP Customer Care position.
B. Director of Engineering—The current Director of Engineering (Erin Suksap) will retire within five years. There is no Star in place for that position. PPP will recruit a Star that can be developed into a Director of Engineering in the future.

C. Inventory Manager—The position is important with over 1,000 SKUs (Stock Keeping Units), high cost of inventory, and customer demands for inventory management. The current person (Bridge O'Dell) is slated for promotion to the VP of Operations within five years. PPP has Doug Harrison, another Star in the pipeline to replace Bridge.
D. Plant Manager—Retirement for this position is unknown. Need to determine specifics and assess succession risk.

Elizabeth comments on the prioritized list. "This shows how vulnerable we are. Many key positions are exposed, including my own. If my father had gone through this exercise, he would have seen that the lack of a good process for succession puts the business at risk. We would have been better prepared if we had a prioritized plan and were thorough and disciplined in our approach."

Treasure 3
Tap The Top Talent

Sage Lesson & Background

John Wooden (1910-2010). Coach Wooden models the importance of paying attention to the right details, using a good process, developing a ritual, and sticking with it for talent recruiting, retention, and succession.

Wooden, an American college basketball coach, won the most NCAA Division I Men's Championships ever (ten in a twelve-year period). He had four undefeated seasons (1964, 1967, 1972, 1973). Wooden was the first person to be inducted into the Basketball Hall of Fame, both as a player (1961) and as a coach (1973). Wooden received the Presidential Medal of Freedom (2003) given by George W. Bush. He was awarded the NCAA Coach of the Century in 2000. He was designated ESPN's Greatest Coach of the 20th Century.

Key Learnings

❏ Tap The Top Talent by paying attention to appropriate details and spending time to **prepare**. Use simple yet effective processes to recruit, retain, and sustain the right talent.

❏ To improve hiring success, **use the Five Steps To Top Talent** process: 1) Front-End The Right Talent Definition; 2) Establish A Magnetic Targeted Network; 3) Optimize Assessment Tools & Techniques; 4) Use A Top-Notch Interview Panel; and 5) Thoroughly Validate Talent.

❏ Spend time upfront to **define** the essential performance metrics, success characteristics and behaviors, and cultural compatibilities (values) for the right top talent.

❏ At least yearly, **identify employees with Star potential--the strategic bench strength**—the highest performing future managers and leaders of the company. Invest time, training, and resources to develop and retain your Stars. Ensure Stars are coached by the best managers. Put Stars in roles where they can leverage their strengths and add the most value to customers and the organization.

❏ Prepare for your future. **Use the Five Steps To Successful Succession** process: 1) Identify Expected Exits & New Positions; 2) Identify Best Current Backup Options; 3) Identify Stars & Timing; 4) Create a Gap List; and 5) Define a Prioritized Plan. Sort succession positions into three prioritized categories (high, medium, and low). High priorities are more critical, vulnerable positions. Assign accountabilities to fill high priority positions first.

❏ Make succession an active part of leadership team meetings, strategic planning, and board meetings. Be disciplined, thorough and intentional. **Update** the succession plan yearly or when key positions unexpectedly depart.

TREASURE

4

OPERATIONAL DISCIPLINE: HELPS YOU WIN

Elizabeth and Joseph hear a lot of commotion. They are in the flywheel magneto assembly area of the Model T automobile plant. The flywheel magneto is a part of the Model T engine. It generates power to the spark plugs. It has sixteen V shaped magnets. They are assembled with bolts to a large round metal flywheel.

Twenty-nine workers are gathered around a new experimental factory setup for the flywheel magneto. They are standing in front of a long three-foot high makeshift structure. The workers are asked to line up along this new "moving" assembly line. It is made from metal pipes and bins. It has a long row of magneto shells sitting along the top. The magneto flywheels can be moved along the line to the individual workers. Underneath in the bins are bolts used for assembly.

The workers are instructed to put on a single V magnet part and bolt it onto the magneto flywheel. After that, the workers are asked to slide (move) the flywheel a few feet to the next worker who will assemble another of the sixteen V magnets (single part). This process continues until all sixteen bolts are attached to the flywheel by sixteen individual workers.

Model T Magneto Flywheel Assembly Line (1913)

This innovative work process (flow) is completely different from the previous method. The day before, each worker had assembled all sixteen parts and the entire flywheel magneto by themselves.

Elizabeth asks a lanky, fiftyish year old man, "What are they experimenting with?" Henry Ford responds, "I believe this is the first moving line ever installed." Elizabeth asks, "Where did the idea come from?" Ford replies, "The idea came in a general way from the overhead trolley that the Chicago packers use in dressing beef."

The date is April 1, 1913. Some workers wonder if this is an April Fool's prank. Henry Ford knows it is not. Elizabeth asks, "Are you going to change the way you assemble the parts?" Ford responds, "We try everything in a little way first—we will rip out anything once we discover a better way, but we have to know absolutely that the new way is going to be better than the old before we do anything drastic."

As Joseph and Elizabeth leave the Model T plant in Highland Park, Michigan he asks Elizabeth, "What do you know about Henry Ford and the moving assembly line?" Elizabeth answers, "Ford created the Model T. Based on what we just witnessed, Ford and his production team pioneered the moving assembly line for manufacturing." Joseph says, "That is correct. They innovated a host of disciplines and activities all driven to lower the cost of manufacturing the automobile."

Joseph continues. "Here is more background. In 1910 there were about 300 horseless-carriage (automobile) manufacturers in the United States. Before Ford's Model T, automobiles were an expensive novelty. Beyond the high initial cost of the automobile, many owners had to hire full time chauffeurs to keep their vehicles in running condition. When the Model T was introduced, there were about 200,000 automobiles in America."

Ford's Recipe for Success

Joseph describes Ford. "Henry Ford was disciplined, hard-working, and persistent. His ambitious nature and strong drive fueled a relentless pursuit to lower the cost to manufacture the automobile. He and his team did this so that the masses could afford one and Ford could sell a ton of them."

Joseph continues, "In every business, there are various strategic choices to be made on the specific operational activities (value chain) that add value and help an organization fulfill its promises to customers. If these activities are well chosen, aligned, and relatively less expensive to deliver, they can add significant competitive advantage. The cumulative effect will lead to more profit. It will create a more defensible competitive position."

Joseph refers to the first Treasure. "Ford defined a dream-statement for his Model T:

'I will build a car for the great multitude. It will be large enough for the family, but small enough for the individual to run and care for. It will be constructed of the best materials, by the best men to be hired, after the simplest designs that modern engineering can devise. But it will be so low in price that no man making a good salary will be unable to own one – and enjoy with his family the blessing of hours of pleasure in God's great open spaces.'

"The Model T differentiated niche offerings that uniquely satisfied customer needs were *reliable, easy to operate, and easy to repair*. Competitors' automobiles were unreliable, hard to operate, and difficult to repair. Ford's offerings were unique and superior to the competition.

"Up until Ford's Model T introduction, the 200,000 automobiles sold in America were to wealthy hobbyists. Ford's strategic customer was different: *the working, middle class family* (*'great multitude'*).

"Ford focused on the low-price segment (*'it will be so low in price that no man making a good salary will be unable to own one'*). He aggressively lowered price to expand the market." Joseph hands Elizabeth a Strategic Playbook diagram with an interpretation of the Ford Model T 3-Keys-Strategy:

Joseph continues, "With the Model T, Ford was focused mainly on the bottom part (denominator) of the CURVE (Customer Unique and Relative Value Equation): Specifically, *what you relatively pay.*

"He saw opportunity to create a bigger market by systematically reducing manufacturing costs and subsequently, price. To accomplish the 'so low in price' dream, Model T operations leveraged continuous production flow, division of labor, interchangeable parts, and reductions in wasted effort.

"Ford did focus on the top part of the CURVE, but mainly around the differentiated offerings of reliable, easy to operate, and easy to repair. Ford ignored needs such as driving performance, comfort, style, and easy financing.

"Let's review a few more Ford facts. In 1909, the price of the Model T was $900. About 19,000 Model T vehicles were sold that year. Fast forward fifteen years to 1924.

Because of an unyielding pursuit for standardization and operational efficiencies, the Model T's price was significantly reduced to $260. Almost 2,000,000 Model T's were made in 1924.

"The moving assembly line experiment was a 'better way.' It was a breakthrough in operational efficiencies. Ford and his production team discovered it in pursuit of his dream. They were looking for ways to improve efficiencies.

"Now the work was brought to the worker. Each worker did specialized and simple tasks. After a year of refinements, about half as many employees were producing the magneto in about 25% of the time (big pace of growth and financial improvements).

"The moving assembly line process was expanded to other parts of the Highland Park Model T plant. Later, highly disciplined workers were building a chassis in about one and a half hours, down from over twelve hours.

"By the time the moving assembly line and other operational efficiency disciplines where expanded throughout the Model T plant, complete vehicles were rolling off the line every ten seconds. Accelerated speed and efficient manufacturing processes helped Henry Ford continue to lower the price of the Model T. It dramatically improved Ford's competitive advantage. It enabled him to realize his Model T dream-statement."

Joseph continues the conversation. "Operational disciplines that reduce costs are essential during recessions. Companies with more efficient value chains will be in a better position when economic conditions turn unfavorable. They will also have an advantage when economic times are good."

Before going to the next stop in their dream-journey, Joseph summarizes his observations. "We witnessed a terrific recipe for initial business success. Ford had excellent clarity as to where he was headed. He had a focused 3-Keys-Strategy. The moving assembly line breakthrough was catalyzed by a clear and compelling dream-statement. The dream became operationalized because Ford was willing to take calculated risks. He and his production team experimented on how to improve efficiencies. They benchmarked and improved on ideas from other industries (meat packing). Ford did not wait for perfect answers. New operational disciplines were quickly tested. Once proven, the better disciplines were expanded. They were leveraged into other production areas.

"These operational efforts in the value chain were all linked to the customer—being able to consistently deliver a product to the customer at a price that he or she could afford. It gave Ford a significant competitive advantage. That advantage would be realized so long as he continued to improve operational disciplines at a pace faster than competition *and* Ford kept up with gravity-shifts, including changing customer needs and competitive options."

Why Increase Pay to $5 a Day?

Joseph and Elizabeth travel forward in time to January 5, 1914. They are still in Highland Park, Michigan. Ford has convened a press conference. A press release is distributed. Elizabeth is given a copy. She reads it to Joseph:

> "The Ford Motor Company, the greatest and most successful manufacturing company in the world, will, on January 12, inaugurate the greatest revolution in the manner of rewards for its workers ever known in the industrial world. At one stroke, it will reduce the hours of labor from nine to eight and add to

> every man's pay a share of the
> profits of the house. The smallest
> amount to be received by any man
> 22 years old and upwards will be
> $5.00 per day. The minimum wage is
> now $2.34 per day of nine hours."

Elizabeth and Joseph return the next day to the Ford Model T plant. It's ten degrees Fahrenheit. Despite the bitter cold, 10,000 people are lined up outside Ford's Highland Park gates, hoping to be hired.

Elizabeth turns to Joseph with a reference to another Treasure, "Looks like Henry Ford understood the importance of Treasure 3 (Tap The Top Talent)."

Joseph responds, "When evaluating new operational disciplines to help you win, consider how they might impact other factors important for success. Ford's new moving assembly line was an operational discipline breakthrough. However, the monotony of simple, repetitive tasks negatively affected turnover (over 300% at its peak). Ford adjusted. In one profound decision, the institution of the $5 a day pay more than doubled the existing factory rate. This greatly lowered turnover. Some even claim it contributed to Ford's dream—more workers now had money to afford a Model T. Ford not only took a bold step towards his dream. He escalated wages elsewhere. He helped create the middle class in America."

Customer Feedback First

On their journey home, Elizabeth asks Joseph, "Henry Ford was relentless in his pursuit to improve operational disciplines and efficiencies. I would like to instill this mindset and install the right operational disciplines at PPP. What is the first step you recommend we take?" Joseph replies, "Begin with the customer. Henry Ford got this right. He was externally focused on lowering the cost of the automobile so that more customers could afford one."

Joseph continues, "Operationally, it is essential that Peak Precision Parts know what is important to strategic customers—what are their requirements for complex medical parts...what are their hierarchy of needs for speed...accuracy...what are their unmet desires? PPP also needs to know how well it is delivering unique value to the customer—how well it stacks up against other customer choices and what are PPP's differentiated offerings?'

Elizabeth responds, "I see the relevance. I buy into the importance of customer feedback for the entire company. To improve operational disciplines specifically, what would you recommend is the best way to learn this information?"

Joseph replies, "Assuming you do not have in-house market research expertise, there are outside experts that can help with research. Voice of the Customer (VOC) research is a good technique. VOC is a process for capturing customer requirements. It produces a detailed set of customer wants and needs. They are organized into a hierarchical structure and then prioritized. For effective VOC, ask the right questions in the right way to the right customers. VOC research typically provides a Net Promoter Score (NPS). It is a valid indicator of loyalty if the research is done properly.

"There are other useful customer research tools and techniques to consider in addition to or instead of VOC. The best way to identify the right research techniques is to front-end the thinking. You do this by *clearly defining your research objectives*. These objectives must be linked to PPP's 3-Keys-Strategy, business goals, and to the dream-statement. Next, determine what you are going to do with the results. Determine what is actionable. Determine what will change, contingent on research results. Ask questions that directly link back to your research objectives.

"One-on-one research is a great way to glean initial customer insights and reactions to operational or other product and service improvement ideas.

"Consider digitally enabled research tools. They are quick, becoming more accurate, and provide useful feedback. For example, mobile ethnography research asks respondents to download a smartphone app. The app allows respondents to create an ongoing multimedia journal of their experiences with your products and services by posting photo, video, audio, and written feedback.

"Once customer feedback is in hand, ensure it is properly scrubbed for usefulness, analyzed, and summarized. Then share it with operations to improve effectiveness."

Lean Forward With Lean Techniques

Continuing the discussion on relentlessly improving operational efficiencies, Joseph introduces Elizabeth to Lean. "Consider Lean manufacturing techniques. Lean is a later generation of what Ford created with the moving assembly line and other efficiency improvements for the Model T. Ford's efficient manufacturing processes worked well with limited product variety. Later, Toyota improved on Ford's approaches to accommodate quick flow, low waste, and product variety.

"The term 'Lean' was coined to describe Toyota's operational disciplines during the late 1980s by a research team headed by Jim Womack, Ph.D., at MIT's International Motor Vehicle Program. The main idea behind Lean is to maximize customer value while minimizing waste. Simply put, Lean means using fewer resources to create more value for customers. While initially developed for manufacturing, Lean can apply to service operations with great success.

"At Peak Precision Parts, focus Lean on critical waste reduction opportunities as perceived by customers. Here is a list of ten operational areas that are good starting places to identify opportunities to reduce waste and costs at PPP." Joseph hands Elizabeth the list from the Strategic Playbook:

Ten Opportunities to Reduce Waste & Costs

1. Wasted human motions and activities.
2. Time.
3. Human capital (labor).
4. Communication (external and internal).
5. Space (manufacturing, warehousing, office, staging, and others).
6. Defects and service errors.
7. Excess or over production.
8. Inventory and scheduling.
9. Transportation and delivery.
10. Warrantees (returns).

Joseph expands his comments on Lean. "After conducting your customer research, have your operations, finance, and innovation teams determine the areas that are costing the customer and your company the most in terms of waste and negative value. Focus attention there.

"Have operations do a cost and benefit analysis before starting a major project. Validate that the improvement area will be worthwhile. Recall what we heard Henry Ford say about testing before making big bets: 'We try everything in a little way first…we have to know absolutely that the new way is going to be better than the old before we do anything drastic.'"

Elizabeth asks Joseph, "What are the pros of implementing Lean?" Joseph replies, "The results Peak Precision Parts can expect to see will depend on where you start and what effort you put into Lean. Many clients have realized significant balance sheet and income statement improvements after implementing Lean. Peak Precision Parts' profit will be higher because of lower manufacturing, overhead, labor, inventory carrying, and delivery costs. With the right level of commitment, planning, and training, results can come relatively fast.

"Lean can help improve your growth pace. It does this by taking out time-consuming waste, steps, and errors. Safety can be enhanced with fewer materials, steps, and less rework. Employee morale can improve—it is more enjoyable to be on a team with fewer errors."

Elizabeth asks Joseph, "Are there cautions or things to watch out for when implementing Lean?" He responds, "There are. First, it is wise to simplify and eliminate low priority products, services, and customers before implementing Lean. We will discuss how to do this in our next dream-journey. This will make Lean easier to implement and it will be far more impactful.

"Second, many people do not like change. However, they do like progress. If Peak Precision Parts has long term employees that are used to manufacturing a certain way, there may be resistance to undertaking Lean. It can take them out of their comfort zones. Remind employees on the importance of keeping Peak Precision Parts competitive.

"Getting proper training is a necessary investment. If you have qualified trainers at PPP, terrific. If not, use outside resources. Clients have had good experience with the American Society for Quality (ASQ, www.asq.org). ASQ is a knowledge-based global community of 75,000 quality professionals. It is an excellent resource for training in Lean and other quality improvement disciplines."

Joseph shares a final caution for implementing Lean. "The main idea behind this Treasure (Operational Discipline: Helps You Win) is the relentless pursuit to lead and drive relative efficiency (cost) gains by establishing the right operational disciplines. Lean is a good approach. Do not rely solely on it. Once you get traction with Lean, look into other approaches to improve efficiencies and lower costs. Consider Six Sigma, capital investments, technology improvements, supplier programs, near-sourcing, outsourcing..."

Value Chain Breakthroughs

Joseph discusses the value chain. "Michael Porter was first to introduce the value chain, an important concept in building competitive advantage. Here is a definition:

> *'The value chain is a high-level model used to describe the full range of activities needed to take a product or service from creation to customer delivery and follow up service. Companies conduct value chain analysis by identifying ways to increase the efficiency of the chain. The overall goal is to deliver maximum relative value for the least relative cost and create a competitive advantage.'*

"Let's examine Peak Precision Parts' value chain. There are six broad activities—create, purchase (raw materials), manufacture, sell, deliver, and service. Each of these activities can positively or negatively shape customer perceptions of value."

Joseph hands Elizabeth a Playbook example of value chain activities for a company similar to Peak Precision Parts:

The Value Chain

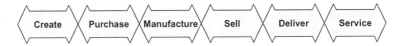

Joseph continues, "This visually shows the broad activities of your value chain. Look at these and the sub-activities. Delineate each broad activity further. For example, *manufacture* typically includes sub-activities such as inventorying raw materials, processing, assembly, packaging, and other activities to make a product.

"Likewise, *create* includes sub-activities such as listening to customers, analyzing needs, determining unique design and product requirements, and so on." Joseph hands Elizabeth a Playbook diagram that breaks out several *create* sub-activities:

CREATE Value Chain Sub-Activities

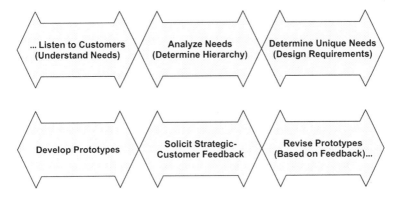

"Evaluate the activities along your value chain—especially where your differentiated niche offerings are most meaningful to customers and your costs are or can be lower than competition."

The Service Value Chain

"Service businesses are growing and omnipresent. Let's discuss the value chain as it relates to service. There are fundamental differences versus manufacturing firms where there is a tangible product that can be made in a controlled environment and inventoried prior to delivery to the customer. Many manufacturing value chain improvements are made to the product before it is delivered to and the customer experiences it.

"In service businesses, there may not be a tangible product that can be premade and inventoried. Value chain improvements typically occur during each stage of customer contact. What the customer uniquely gets and relatively pays (CURVE) is often dependent on the quality and cost of service providers—people who directly deliver the service experience to customers. Look closely at these employees. They can be critical in the service value chain. Identify ways to increase the effectiveness and efficiency of front-line employees to deliver maximum relative value for the least relative cost.

"Now that you have a preliminary understanding of the value chain, let's talk about how to leverage it. Start by isolating strategically relevant activities where you can win—the sources of competitive advantage that can positively affect the CURVE and 3-Keys-Strategy. For instance, identifying faster, more accurate, and lower cost ways of developing prototypes will directly support Peak Precision Parts' 3-Keys-Strategy. Switching to a hospitality industry example, the service value chain can be improved through unique and superior employee selection and training processes. This is especially true for first points of human contact at the hotel (parking attendants, baggage and door assistants, registration desk and concierge employees).

Value Chain Breakthroughs

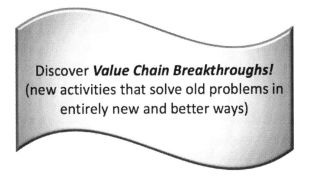

Discover *Value Chain Breakthroughs!* (new activities that solve old problems in entirely new and better ways)

Joseph reveals an important opportunity to maximize competitive advantage and overall success. "In manufacturing and service businesses, a key to winning is uncovering value chain breakthroughs. These are the right strategic activities where you want to become deeply immersed in problem identification. These are the breakthrough opportunities where you discover *new* activities that solve old problems in entirely new and better ways — what Henry Ford's moving assembly line did for the Model T and what Amazon's ordering process did for its online businesses (resulting in lower cost, more efficient service, and fewer errors).

"Value chain breakthroughs bring you closer to realizing an absolute advantage — an ideal state where customers do not emotionally or rationally consider other choices."

Follow The Money

"Let's talk about relative costs in the value chain." Joseph hands Elizabeth another Playbook diagram and discusses it. "In this example, competition's costs are represented by the dashed line:

Value Chain Relative Cost Differences

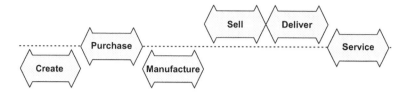

"As you can see, several components of this value chain example have higher relative costs than competition (sell and deliver activities are depicted above the dashed line). They hurt competitive advantage. Two have lower relative costs (create and manufacture are below the dashed line). They help competitive advantage. Two are equal (purchase of raw materials and service). They have no effect on competitive advantage.

"Follow the money. Find areas where your costs are or can be low relative to competition. If you can perform a different or better activity, or the same activity at a lower cost in any of these areas, you gain an advantage. In service industries, focus on front-line talent (investment, training, and quality) and technology solutions that can provide superior service at a lower cost.

"Fixed assets and technology can affect the value chain. Companies that compete in heavy asset-based or technology dependent industries know this. This includes equipment-based and software-based service businesses. Allocations for equipment, technology, and other fixed assets can be critical to delivering superior value and financial performance. Identify opportunities to gain value chain advantages by carefully selecting then leveraging fixed assets and innovative technology solutions.

"Sourcing parts, materials, and services from suppliers is another area that is important to consider within the value chain. Determine how much leverage suppliers have over you, and vice-versa. Is it easy for suppliers to drive up prices that you pay for critical cost components? How abundant or scarce are quality suppliers? Ensure a qualified person at Peak Precision Parts is paying attention to supplier leverage. Have them properly trained in negotiations."

Elizabeth asks how to obtain information on relative competitive costs. "We have several large competitors. They probably have lower costs than us due to scale. How do you suggest we learn what our competitors' costs are?" Joseph replies, "Just because a competitor is larger does not mean that they have lower costs. A lot of large companies suffer from overhead creep. Many companies become complacent about cost efficiencies. Superior utilization of resources can be achieved in mid and small companies.

"Start by prioritizing your top competitors as perceived by potential strategic customers. Ask customers for their perceptions. Use direct observation. Evaluate your competitors' products and services. Reverse engineer their products and services.

"Review competitor websites, marketing, pricing, and promotion materials. Look at reference databases, published news articles, and press releases. If the competitor is a public company, read their annual reports and 10K documents. If the competitor is going public, look at their S1 documents.

"Trade associations may have insight. Go to trade shows. Find former employees that are not bound by non-compete agreements. Learn from and leverage networks—anyone that ethically can provide accurate information on competitive costs. Assign accountabilities within PPP to honorably obtain competitive costs—especially in areas that are strategically important to you."

The Right Start

"The value chain requires analysis and detailed work. You want to keep turning over the right rocks to discover the best opportunities (breakthroughs) to improve value (CURVE). This is a continuing effort. Keep digging to identify strategic areas which can provide you the best ROI if pursued. Focus on areas that are already differentiated. Every cost should add value to the end-use customer. If not significant, do you outsource? If significant, do you vertically integrate? Investigate how each activity can be turned into an advantage."

Elizabeth asks, "There is much to tackle to improve our value chain...how do we start?" Joseph replies, "Here is a list of the right questions to help you and your team get off to the right start." Joseph hands Elizabeth the questions from the Strategic Playbook:

Value Chain: The Right Questions

o What are important activities (broad and sub) in your value chain (write them down)?
   ▪ Which are most important to strategic customers and support the 3-Keys-Strategy best (prioritize them)?
   ▪ These are the strategic activities and opportunities where you want to discover value chain breakthroughs—new activities that solve old problems in entirely new and better ways (similar to Ford's moving assembly line).
o Which are least important (you can't do everything, don't hedge your bets—say no)?
o Which do you already have relative advantages?
o Which build the best walls for sustainable competitive advantages?
o Which require the least effort to improve the CURVE the most?

- What fixed assets can improve the value chain the most with the least investment?
- What win-win supplier activities can help you achieve greater leverage and value to customers?
- What is the ROI to pursue the above?
- Who is specifically accountable to do what and by when?
    - What are the most important objectives and key results that should be led?

Joseph finishes his value chain teachings: "Remember, it's about strategic differences. To paraphrase Porter (*Competitive Advantage*) and Joan Magretta (*Understanding Michael Porter*) and using the Playbook's definition of value, it is a difference in relative needs (what customers uniquely and relatively get—the top part of the CURVE) and relative costs (what customers relatively pay—the bottom part of the CURVE) that arises because of differences in the activities being performed. Net, it's about superior differences in how the company performs the right activities that result in improving the CURVE. These differences lead to true competitive advantage.

"To conclude, the value chain is a valuable way to look at your business. Recall our visits with Henry Ford. His passion to lower costs throughout the Model T value chain led to breakthrough reductions in price. It led to a competitive advantage. You want to continually evaluate and determine if there are material differences between your activities and cost structures relative to competitors. Then make the right strategic choices to build your advantages."

As the Wheel Turns

After Joseph departs from their Henry Ford dream-journey, Elizabeth looks through the *Ten Treasures Strategic Playbook* presentation and reads more about Ford:

Ford Gravity-Shifts & Niches

Every activity Ford pursued in the manufacture of the Model T was intended to lower the cost and price of the vehicle. Over time, the Model T price dropped from $900 to $260. In total, more than 15 million were made.

While Ford's Model T was a remarkable success for nearly twenty years, gravity-shifts changed the game, but not in Ford's favor. Ford lost top talent (Stars) to competitors who introduced his production disciplines into their operations. Ford's initial focus on operational efficiencies served him well until competitors niched the new and offered customers more unique choices (top part of the CURVE).

Competitors developed differentiated 3-Keys-Strategies. Initial differentiators included style, comfort, and financing (buying a car on credit). Later, cars had more power, better driving performance, improved safety, ease-of-driving... These unique strategies diluted Ford's market share. In 1925, General Motors surpassed Ford in revenues, a position it maintained until 1986.

Summary point: the antidotes to these gravity-shifts could have been realized if Ford successfully revisited Treasure 1 (Define The Dream) and applied Treasure 2 (Niche The New).

Another unexpected gravity-shift occurred on October 29, 1929. During the Great Depression, Ford sales dropped 50%. It lost about $75 million in 1932. At this point in time, the industry had consolidated to the Big Three (Ford, GM, and Chrysler).

The Big Three dominance continued until the Japanese invasion in the 1960's (gravity-shift). Japanese auto companies initially differentiated with low-price (bottom part of the CURVE), smaller, and fuel efficient automobiles. Over time, they concentrated on customer research, product quality, and pursued Lean and other operational disciplines that led to superior quality and reliability. Eventually, they niched into the high price segment with separate upscale brands (Lexus, Acura, Infiniti).

Today, the auto wheels continue to turn with new niches in ride-sharing, self-driving, connectivity, sustainability, safety...

Elizabeth recalls the gravity-shifts lesson in Treasure 2. It had such a clear message. She says to herself, "We must leverage gravity-shifts, watch out for complacency, and continue to innovate at Peak Precision Parts."

Treasure 4
Operational Discipline:
Helps You Win

Sage Lesson & Background

Henry Ford (1863-1947). Ford teaches the value of intentionally and strategically pursuing the right operational disciplines to deliver a lower relative cost and improve competitive advantage.

Ford was an American industrialist who pioneered disciplined and efficient operational processes. Ford's moving assembly line and mass production techniques revolutionized the automobile value equation. He transformed the automobile from a high-priced curiosity into an everyday transportation convenience. As a result, Ford helped reengineer social life in the United States of America.

Key Learnings

❑ Develop and improve operational disciplines that **reduce costs, waste, and errors relative to competition**. The right execution and operational disciplines significantly strengthen the CURVE and competitive advantage. Manufacturing and service companies with the most efficient processes and best disciplines will be in better financial shape when economic conditions turn unfavorable.

❑ Improving operational disciplines (and efficiencies) starts with **objective customer research** and feedback. Learn customer requirements, desires, and their hierarchy of needs (versus other choices). Analyze, summarize, and share relevant findings.

❑ **Test new operational disciplines**. Once proven, expand the better disciplines broadly. Develop methods to do this quickly yet accurately.

❑ **Leverage Lean techniques** to strategically and systematically reduce waste. Find the highest waste areas as perceived by customers and focus attention there.

❑ Improving the value chain requires analysis and detailed work. **Continually look** at broad and sub-activities of the value chain to identify the best opportunities to improve value. **Isolate strategically relevant activities**—the sources of competitive advantage that can positively affect the CURVE, 3-Keys-Strategy and build competitive walls. Ask the right value chain questions to help you and your team get off to the right start.

❑ To maximize competitive advantage and overall success, **discover value chain breakthroughs**—new activities that solve old problems in entirely new and better ways.

❑ Service business value chain improvements typically occur during customer contact. Identify ways to **increase effectiveness and efficiencies of front-line employees** to deliver maximum relative value for the least relative cost.

TREASURE

5

ELEVATE THE ELEPHANTS

Before Joseph begins their fifth adventure, Elizabeth refers to PPP's Competitive Comparison Questions survey results. "As I recall, the question, 'How well does PPP prioritize (focus on the important, say no to the less important), relative to competition' was the fifth lowest score. This is our fifth dream-journey. Coincidence?" Joseph responds. "No. Good observation. We are pursuing the dream-journeys in the order of the Competitive Comparison Question results—lowest to highest.

"Tonight, we will be making a brief visit to Switzerland. After that, most of this dream-journey will be in your home. We will discuss an infrequently used Treasure. It can be very valuable to Peak Precision Parts. That is, if you understand its power and learn how to use it properly."

In a flash, they are in Lausanne, Switzerland. The year is 1906. They witness a well-dressed professor with dark hair, a distinguished mustache, and full beard. He is in a large office filled with sociology, math, history, and reference books.

The professor is pouring over calculations and mathematical models. He is plotting out wealth distribution graphs with a pencil. He is connecting data points that correlate the Italian population with wealth. Elizabeth notices that the series of graphs have similar patterns.

Elephants Rule (80/20)

Elizabeth has no time to fully grasp what she saw. They are instantly back in her home. Joseph starts talking, "The person we briefly visited was Vilfredo Pareto. Pareto was an Italian economist and sociologist. The graphs we saw him working on showed that a small percent of the Italian population (20%) possessed most of the wealth (80%). Sadly, Pareto was not a very good story teller. So, the great work we witnessed, and Pareto's brilliant findings were mostly unknown. That is, until a quality guru named Joseph Juran rediscovered Pareto."

"Juran coined the term, 'The Pareto Principle.' The 'Pareto' name stuck. It has become the name associated with a significant, universal principle. Specifically, the concept that a limited number of inputs, causes, and efforts (the 20%) lead to most of the outputs, results, and rewards (the 80%)."

Elephants First

Joseph transitions to storytelling mode. "Not sure who the author is, but this story captures the essence of Pareto's Principle:

> 'If you're Noah and your ark is about to sink, *look for the elephants first*, because you can throw over a bunch of cats, dogs, squirrels, and everything else that is just a small animal and your ark will keep sinking. But if you can find one elephant to get overboard, you're in much better shape.'"

Joseph shares another elephant analogy. He refers Elizabeth to the popular *elephant in the room* idiom. "As you know, this metaphor is about a big problem of which everyone is aware, but no one wants to talk about. In our case, elephants are the *biggest (most important) opportunities that we want to find and elevate*, not the big problems that we want to hide and put aside.

"This begs a question. In business, why doesn't leadership consistently elevate the elephants (focus on the biggest opportunities)? One reason many organizations do not elevate the elephants is because they spend too much time chasing smaller animals. They fixate on familiar, less important activities—not necessarily the right ones. They do not want to leave their comfort zones.

"In other cases, leadership may see the elephants, but they do not know how to elevate and leverage them, so they ignore them.

"There is a third reason leadership does not effectively elevate the elephants: They do not effectively lead and say 'no.'

"A key to success in business is choosing what not to do (choosing what to avoid). This requires a mindset to help you identify what is important and what's not. Many businesses fail to succeed because they take on too much. They manage with many 'exceptions.' They do not effectively differentiate between more and less important tasks and priorities.

"Everyone in business can be more successful by following the elephant's rule: *focus on the most important; say NO to everything else!* This changes where you direct your attention. It is a better way of thinking about your business. It is a better way of leading your business. Elevating the elephants leads to more effective and efficient results. It leads you to success. Joseph hands Elizabeth an image from the Strategic Playbook:

Elevate The Elephants

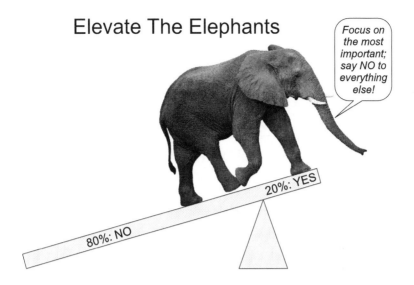

"It is easy to say no to the trivial. It is a leader's job to say no to good opportunities that are not the most important. Saying no to everything but the most important separates great strategy from good strategy. It separates great leaders from mediocre leaders. To master elevating the elephants, you must relentlessly say no to everything but the most important."

Joseph continues, "Leaders, and for that matter, everyone in business should continuously ask:

> *'What is the biggest elephant I can elevate with the least effort to realize the best return on my effort?'"*

Joseph presents an opinion. "Often the most successful people know how to focus on simple yet profound ideas. This is an uncommon ability. It is harder to do than it appears. Martin Luther King Jr. did this with his *I Have a Dream* message. Steve Jobs simplified product innovation. Coach Wooden codified his approach to top talent into a pyramid. Ford simplified manufacturing techniques. Vilfredo Pareto presented extensive wealth distribution data in graphs that validated the 80/20 concept."

80/20 Facts & Focus

"Before we go on, let's summarize—Pareto uncovered the principle. Juran broadened and branded it. It is one of the best kept secrets of highly successful organizations and leaders. A key way to leverage 80/20 is to elevate the elephants. This focus starts by asking what is the biggest elephant you can leverage with the least effort to realize the best return on your effort."

Elizabeth asks, "I assume it doesn't have to precisely be an 80/20 ratio?" Joseph replies, "Correct. 80/20 is a guideline. Depending on the circumstances, the actual ratio may be 70/30, 90/10, 50/5, 52/3, or even 50/1. Regardless of the exact ratio, the directional power of 80/20 is the same—a small amount of effort (resources) drives most of the success. The converse is true—a large amount of effort (resources) can produce few or negative results."

Joseph shares a range of interesting facts and examples of the Pareto Principle from the Strategic Playbook:

Examples of The Pareto Principle (80/20)

o 20% of active Major League Baseball players hit 77% of total home runs (2017 MLB data).
o 20% of the roads driven on carry most of the automobile traffic.
o 20% of patients use most of the healthcare resources.
o 20% of criminals commit most of the crimes.
o 16.5% of US individual federal income tax returns paid 79.4% of the total federal income taxes (2014 IRS data, Pew Research Center).
o 10% of companies with sales greater than $1 billion generate 80% of the profit (McKinsey Global Institute "Superstars" paper, October 2018, n = 5,750 companies).

- 10% of the world's countries (twenty) generate 80% of the world's GDP (2017 International Monetary Fund data).
- 10% of alcohol drinkers consume about half the alcohol.
- 5% of the population represent over half of lottery ticket revenues.
- 1% of registered website domain names are estimated to generate more than 95% of total internet traffic (data estimated based on 330 million registered websites in 2017).

Joseph proceeds by asking Elizabeth to evaluate her personal situations. "Take your cell phone calls. If you're like most people, 20% or fewer of your contacts represent 80% or more of your calls. Same goes for emails, text messages, what you wear, what rooms you spend time in your home, where you eat your meals, and with whom you spend your time."

Joseph redirects the conversation back to business. "Businesses are one of the most fertile areas for elevating elephants (leveraging the power of Pareto). Look at where your revenues and profits come from. You will likely find elephants in the form of target customer prospects, product (service) innovation opportunities, manufacturing costs, inventories, quality defects, employee performance, turnover—the list goes on."

Elephant Advantages

"Elevating the elephants makes work easier and more enjoyable. That's because it eliminates wasted, unproductive, and frustrating activities. Elevating the elephants refocuses energy, resources, and people on the best opportunities for success. Elevating the elephants can significantly strengthen the CURVE (Customer Unique and Relative Value Equation). It can improve competitive advantage, and subsequently, profitability. More profit means more potential."

Elizabeth asks, "So, on how many 'elephants' do successful leaders focus?" Joseph responds. "There isn't a magic number. With that said, most successful leaders excel at paring down priorities to the handful that really matter. Gravity-shifts, resources, customer choices, competitors, and other important variables will change over time. Priorities must evolve too. Successful leaders become masters at elevating the elephants—they focus on the right priorities and adjust them at the right time."

Elizabeth comments, "I can think of one priority I'd like to evolve. Elevating the elephants can help me renegotiate the bank covenants as Peak Precision Parts continues to improve profits."

Matter of Facts

Joseph smiles and suggests: "A good starting point to elevate the elephants is to learn and understand the facts. Then define the most important problem you are trying to solve or the most important opportunity you are interested in pursuing (the biggest elephant). A poorly defined problem or opportunity will likely result in poor results. Once the essential problem or opportunity is properly defined, then ask the question:

> *'What is the biggest elephant I can elevate with the least effort to realize the best return on my effort?'*

"Focus on the few activities, inputs, and costs that result in the most return. Likewise, identify the majority activities, inputs, and costs that are not delivering results. Scale them back, redirect, or better yet, eliminate them completely— say no. Focus on the highest payoff opportunities that require the least amount of effort."

Loaded Dice

"Here's a good quote by professor Joseph Ford. He taught physics and specialized in chaos theory at the Georgia Institute of Technology:

> 'God plays dice with the universe. But they're loaded dice. And the main objective is to find out by what rules they are loaded and how we can use them for our own ends.'"

Joseph continues, "As we learned from the game of Monopoly, the Jail (visiting) square is landed on most. This little understood but useful fact provides the knowledgeable player with an advantage in playing the game." Joseph advises, "Proper analysis is essential to find out how the dice are loaded. Learn and use facts. They are our friends. Seek to understand truth."

Playing Smart

"Always look for an elephant advantage before approaching a project or activity. Evaluate and adjust priorities, accordingly. Manage for results. Allocate resources to the most important opportunities, not problems.

"Once the opportunities are flushed out and the best options identified, the next step is to identify major constraints. Sort constraints into an 80/20 framework. Analyze the top 'elephant' constraints first."

Elizabeth reveals, "I see that elevating the elephants company-wide can have a big impact. I thought I understood 80/20. My predisposition to treat everyone the same may have biased my thinking. It will require me to change and play a smarter game. The playing field can still be fair. However, it does not have to be level."

Customers Are Not Equal

Elizabeth asks, "I would like your help as to where and how to begin to elevate the elephants at Peak Precision Parts." Joseph immediately pivots to a favorite form of teaching—asking the right questions. Joseph asks, "How many total customers does Peak Precision Parts have?" She responds, "About 500."

Good Customers

"What about good customers?" A discussion ensues. They make a list of what defines good PPP customers (this assessment will vary by company):

Peak Precision Parts' Good Customer Criteria

o   Good customers want outsourced medical device products from PPP that are perceived to be equal or directionally superior to competition.
o   Low price is not the main buying consideration.
o   There is a fair amount of business (at least $500,000 in revenues a year). The business is profitable (25% or greater gross profit margin).
o   Sales has access to decision makers.

After they are reasonably satisfied with criteria for "good customers," Joseph asks, "How many Peak Precision Parts' customers would you say are good customers?" She responds, "Off the top of my head, about fifty."

Strategic Customers

Joseph begins a conversation about strategic customers. "These are the *true elephants*. We discussed strategic customers when we talked through your preliminary 3-Keys-Strategy in Treasure 2 (Niche The New).

"These are the existing customers you are going to nurture and delight, in other words, strive for customer intimacy. They are the most important customer prospects you are going to target. These are the carefully chosen customers that represent the absolute best strategic bets."

Discussion ensues about what is a strategic customer. This takes considerably more time to define than a "good customer." After thinking, discussion, and mind-sweat, Joseph and Elizabeth write down a list of specific criteria that define a Peak Precision Parts' strategic customer. The list includes choosing to allocate top resources and giving priority treatment to strategic customers:

Peak Precision Parts' Strategic Customer Criteria & Focus

- o Strategic customers desire outsourced solutions for complex, mission-critical parts (CMCP). PPP's products are perceived to be unique, meaningful, and superior to competitive offerings. They are centered around the differentiated niche offerings of *speed* and *accuracy*.
- o PPP knows the strategic customer intimately. Sales and other executives have excellent relationships with decision makers. PPP knows who the influencers and gatekeepers are. Sales and other PPP employees have good relationships with at least twenty people at each strategic customer. Considerable time is spent understanding and solving strategic customer problems.
- o Low price is less important than other benefits. Gross profit margins are 30% or higher. Annual revenues exceed $5 million.
- o There is a win-win, mutually profitable relationship. Information is shared both ways. Feedback flows both ways. Complaints are given in the spirit of continual improvement. There is co-earned loyalty, trust, and respect for each other's values.

o There is future growth opportunity. Strategic customers are important contributors to achieving Peak Precision Parts' TRUE (Tied-to-profit, Risk-aligned, Unmistakable, Explosive) goal.
o PPP will prioritize strategic customers above all others. It will allocate the best resources and talent on strategic customer business. It will develop the right systems and processes to consistently deliver on strategic customer experiences.

After they are satisfied with the high standards for strategic customers, they update the Peak Precision Parts 3-Keys-Strategy definition. Joseph then asks: "How many Peak Precision Parts customers would you say are strategic customers?" Elizabeth responds, "Sadly, only a handful: perhaps five."

Joseph makes a prediction. "Peak Precision Parts' fifty good customers (which include its five strategic customers), represent about 10% of total customers (500 divided by 50). Assuming your guesstimates are correct, I predict that these 10% of total customers will contribute as much as 100% of your profits. This would be a 100/10 ratio."

Surprised, Elizabeth confesses, "We never looked at our customers this way. My father always preached that the customer came first, regardless of size, potential, profitability, or any other factor. He treated all customers the same. This is a profoundly different way to look at customers and our business."

No-Customers

Joseph and Elizabeth look at the other side of the coin. They make a list of what defines a "no" customer:

Peak Precision Parts' No-Customer Criteria

o No-customers do not fit the 3-Keys-Strategy. There is limited or no alignment with PPP's future strategic direction. No-customers will likely not value future PPP strategic product or service offerings.

o No-customers perceive PPP's products as commodities. There are reasonably close substitutes available (as perceived by no-customers).

o Low price is typically a main consideration. PPP realizes less than $100,000 in revenue a year from each no-customer. PPP realizes less than a 25% gross profit margin.

o PPP has wasted time and effort selling no-customers with the "hope" that someday they will contribute more volume. Fact is, there is no future opportunity. More importantly, PPP is making little or no profit (after all overheads and expenses are allocated).

o PPP spends considerable time and resources attempting to "please" no-customers. Many of the complaints and unsatisfied customers are in the no-customer camp (20/80 based on complaints).

Joseph suggests that the approximate 450 no-customers are likely consuming considerable resources — from sales, operations, customer service, inventory, accounts receivable, and other areas within PPP.

Joseph makes another prediction. "If all costs to create, manufacture, sell, deliver, and service are properly allocated to these 450 no-customers, Peak Precision Parts is likely *losing* money on them. I suggest you and your team challenge the status quo and get the facts. Do the proper analysis to discover truth.

"Equally important to losing money, you are wasting considerable, precious resources. I would hazard a guess that some of your best talent is consumed trying to improve a losing battle with no-customers.

"Here's the point that matters: *PPP has too few strategic customers. Wouldn't it be smarter to reinvest top sales talent towards prospecting and developing more strategic customers?* If you doubled the number of strategic customers from five to ten, you will be much more profitable. Reinvest and focus on the most important strategic customer prospects. Ignore the no-customers. Likewise, reinvest operations, customer service, and other talent towards retaining your existing strategic customers. Consistently deliver on their experiences."

Gracefully Let No-Customers Go

Elizabeth asks, "What do we do with the no-customers?" Joseph responds, "Analyze and develop a numerically prioritized or tiered list (worst to best) of all customers. Then gracefully let go the no-customers in the order of the prioritized list. Identify a leader to manage the transition carefully. As you transition, it's best to honor everything you have previously committed to. Reset expectations going forward. Avoid burning bridges."

Products (Services)?

Joseph explains that elevating the elephants is consistent with a fundamental principle of success in warfare. He quotes Frederick the Great. "He who attempts to defend everywhere defends nothing."

Joseph explains, "In business as in warfare, you cannot attack or defend everywhere. Do not hedge your bets by developing products that attempt to appeal to everyone. Avoid all 'exceptions' unless they truly support the 3-Keys-Strategy and strategic customer needs."

Joseph continues to explore where to find and elevate additional elephants. He asks Elizabeth about PPP's products (he notes that the same questioning applies to services). "How many products does Peak Precision Parts have?" Elizabeth responds, "Not sure about the number of products. However, we have over 1,000 SKUs (Stock Keeping Units). This figure was brought up last week by Bridge O'Dell, our inventory manager. She was concerned because we need to update our inventory management software because of the ever-increasing number of SKUs...I see where you are going with your *right question*. Yes, only a critical few products are contributing the most to our profitability."

Knowing that Elizabeth is a quick study, Joseph skips ahead to this statement. "You now know the questions to take back to your leadership team. Would it be helpful to draft a list of criteria for PPP no-products?" Elizabeth responds, "Yes. That would be great. Thank you."

They discuss potential criteria and refine them. They then create a list of guidelines for no-products. This list will help the leadership team pare down the 1,000 plus PPP SKUs. Joseph comments on the list. "It will reduce inventories and resources to purchase, track, and warehouse the SKUs. PPP's cash flow will improve by eliminating the appropriate no-products. It will guide future product development." Here is their list:

Peak Precision Parts' No-Products Criteria

o   No-products are not strategic to PPP. There is limited or no alignment with the 3-Keys-Strategy and dream-statement. No-products are not complex, mission-critical parts—centered around the differentiated niche offerings of speed and accuracy.
o   Strategic customers do not value no-products. They are not differentiated. The product or SKU is perceived to be a commodity. There are readily available substitutes at comparable or lower price points. They do not

require much skill (low value-add). They are easily outsourced or subcontracted.

○ There is low or no net profit. The company may even lose money on no-products. Sales volume is low (less than $25,000 in revenues a year per product SKU).

○ No-products are typically exceptions, custom, or one-off products. They will never sell in high quantities. There is limited future potential.

Carefully Let No-Products Go

Joseph recommends that PPP develop a prioritized or tiered list (worst to best) of all its product lines and SKUs. Joseph cautions, "Unlike no-customers, carefully analyze customer cross purchases before eliminating no-products. If you decide to cut out some low yield products or SKUs, you may lose good or strategic customers who want the convenience of shopping with one supplier: Peak Precision Parts."

Joseph continues, "Take a retail grocery store as an example. A good or strategic customer may shop at the grocery store and want to purchase the low profit products along with highly profitable strategic-products. If you eliminate low profit products, some of your good and strategic customers may think about shopping elsewhere.

"The lesson: do your homework. Get the data and analyze the facts. Be careful. Understand if there are important cross-links among good and strategic customer needs and requirements for all your products and SKUs. Keep the no-products (and SKUs) that strategic customers want to purchase from you. Don't be penny wise and product foolish."

Questionable Priorities

After discussing PPP's customers and products, Joseph presents Elizabeth with an extensive list of additional questions about priorities from the Playbook.

Elizabeth plans to take this list to her leadership team. She will have them delete, add to, edit, and *prioritize* it, as appropriate. After that, data and analysis will support the right actionable plans. This will begin an ongoing journey of elevating the elephants at Peak Precision Parts.

<u>Elevate The Elephant</u>
<u>Questions & Opportunities</u>

Leadership & Strategy

- o What is the most important decision to successfully lead the company to greatness (including what to say no to)?
- o What are the most important goals—long and short term?
- o What is the biggest obstacle or constraint that is holding the company back from achieving its dream-statement and its long-term (TRUE) goal? What are the most important consequences of not removing the biggest obstacle or constraint?
- o Which projects can most rapidly accelerate the growth rate with existing resources and the least amount of effort?
- o What gravity-shifts are most important that can affect future success?
- o Which new strategic product (service) innovations are most important to pursue?
- o What are the most effective strategies and tactics to build competitive advantage?

Tap The Top Talent

- What is the single most important skill that, if you fully developed it, can have the biggest impact on your future success?
- What new hire is most important to the organization's future success?
- Who are the right top talent, the Stars—the top 10% that will contribute to and drive 90% of the value creation?
- Who are the low performing talent? Are they worth saving? Can they be retrained?
- Who are the most effective coaches within the organization?
- What training approaches and materials are most effective?
- What talent improvement methods are most effective?
- Who are the most effective interviewers?
- What interviewing questions are most effective?
- What talent screening tools are most effective?
- What roles are most important to pay attention to with regards to succession?

Sales & Marketing

- What networking opportunities can open the best doors to strategic customer prospects?
- What points of customer contact are most and least important?
- What are the most effective ways to improve customer perceptions of value, relative to competition?
- What marketing message is most persuasive from the strategic customers' perspective?
- What are the highest ROI ways to effectively reach prospective strategic customers?

Operations & Finance
- o Where are the value chain breakthrough opportunities?
- o What operational processes are most and least important to the customer and company (relative to competition)?
- o What is the most important cost reduction opportunity to pursue?
- o What capital investment will provide the highest return (ROI)?
- o What is the best way to leverage the company's financial resources?
- o What is the best opportunity to improve cash flow?

Culture & Other
- o What are the biggest obstacles to realizing a healthy culture?
- o How can PPP culturally get workers to stop doing work that is a waste of time?
- o What existing policies are most important?
- o What employee communications are most important?
- o What is the most effective way to align employees?
- o What is the most effective way to improve accountability?
- o What areas of intentional improvement will provide the best return on effort?
- o What technology solutions can have the greatest impact on the company's future success with the least investment in total resources?
- o Where else within PPP can a small amount of effort pay the biggest dividends with the best return on effort?

After looking through the list, Elizabeth proclaims, "It's clear that elevating the elephants can be deployed virtually everywhere." Joseph agrees and advises, "It must become a cultural norm to work consistently. Have it permeate thinking and behaviors throughout the company. Consider it for every project and activity. Make it *everybody's business*."

Joseph summarizes a major benefit of elevating the elephants for Peak Precision Parts. "This underutilized Treasure is a profit accelerator. It alone can contribute much to Peak Precision Parts' profit turnaround."

Joseph reminds Elizabeth that, "A genuine elevating the elephants effort requires analysis to properly set priorities. It takes commitment from leadership and the team to say no to realize its full potential. Statements such as *'every customer prospect is a good customer and every order is a good order'* are contradictory to elevating the elephants."

Yes, No, & Gray Zones

Joseph discusses a conceptual tool called Yes, No, & Gray Zones. "This can help with identifying, setting, and refining priorities."

To help understand Yes, No, & Gray Zones, Joseph shares a visual from the Playbook. It has three concentric circles that form three areas:

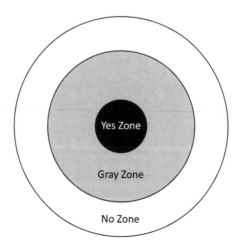

Joseph explains, "The smallest, black, innermost area is labeled the Yes Zone. The Yes Zone represents the most important priorities (the 20% that will drive 80% of the results). This includes strategic customers, strategic products, strategic services, Star employees, and the other inputs, causes, and efforts that produce most of the outputs, results, and rewards."

Joseph continues teaching, "The largest, white, outer-most area is called the No Zone. The No Zone represents the least important priorities (the 80% of efforts that will deliver 20% or fewer of the results). This includes no-customers, no-products, no-services, and other low priorities that need to be eliminated or not pursued (avoided).

"The middle or gray area is called the Gray Zone." Joseph explains, "You can never know everything. Everyone must work with some uncertainty or 'gray' area. The Gray Zone includes priorities that are unclear (fuzzy). They should be analyzed and better defined. The objective is to move unclear priorities from the Gray Zone into either the Yes or the No Zone when data, analysis, and wisdom support a move."

Eliminate The Gray Zone

Joseph hands Elizabeth another visual from the Playbook. The Gray Zone is much smaller in this illustration. The Yes and No Zones are larger:

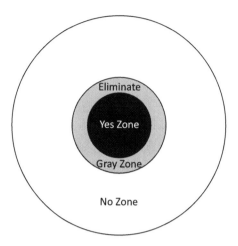

Josephs succinctly says, "This is what good 80/20 looks like. There are few fuzzy priorities. Most of the priorities are defined and clear. Accurately define, analyze, and eliminate the Gray Zone. Know the truth. Secure the most reliable, revealing information. Strip away important uncertainties."

Joseph explains, "Pay attention. Understand and identify (recognize) what are uncertain priorities. That is where improvement can occur, especially if the Gray Zone materially affects outcomes."

Joseph describes the optimizing, tweaking, and fine-tuning processes and efforts to create a great 3-Keys-Strategy as a form of getting rid of the Gray Zone. He brings up other examples where it's important to eliminate uncertainties. "Really well-defined role descriptions will have a small Gray Zone. Same goes for the hiring processes, selecting and qualifying the right new product or service innovations, identifying strategic customers, the list goes on. In all of these examples, analysis and optimization have resulted in less fuzziness and fewer uncertain priorities. There is a small, narrow Gray Zone."

Joseph suggests starting with the obvious: "Define the Yes Zone. Then define the No Zone. Lastly, identify the Gray Zone as best you can." He reiterates, "Keep refining and eliminating the Gray. Analyze. Edit. Cull. Weed out until mostly the Yes and No Zones remain. It's a never-ending journey. That's because we will never know everything. There will always be some uncertainty—some gray area between the yes and no areas. However, we can analyze, better define, and improve by reducing the important Gray Zone areas."

Elephant Traction

Elizabeth asks Joseph, "Do you have suggestions to increase the odds that elevate the elephants gets traction at Peak Precision Parts?" Joseph responds, "To make elevate the elephants more actionable and accountable, add specific time frames when asking questions. For example, 'What is the biggest elephant I can elevate today with the least effort to realize the best return on today's effort?' The specific time period can be adjusted from short to long. For example, you can insert: today; this month; this year…to the question. Alternatively, insert a specific date: 'by (fill in blank) date.'"

Elizabeth thanks Joseph for the tip. It brings up another concern: "Elevating elephants makes so much sense. But it's unlikely we can take it on broadly without adequate help and training." Joseph responds, "Excellent point. Your instincts are on target, there is a lot to it. There are outside 80/20 resources that can help you with training and implementation. Investigate those options and find one that works for you."

Joseph adds another important point. "Elevate the elephants will require a change in Peak Precision Parts' culture. To effectively gain traction with elevate the elephants, it is essential that you (as President) and the leadership team embrace the cultural change and fully support the elevate the elephants implementation.

"Changing the culture and establishing a mindset of elevating the elephants begins with asking the right questions. It continues with the right training, analysis, and a cultural shift. It requires responsibility to make difficult but prudent decisions. It requires leadership.

"As a result, there will be a larger No Zone, a more important Yes Zone, and a shrinking Gray Zone. The end result will be more profit from fewer resources in less time…and more profit means more potential."

Treasure 5
Elevate The Elephants

Sage Lesson & Background

Vilfredo Federico Damaso Pareto (1848-1923). Pareto introduces an important and powerful concept for business success: 80/20. Joseph redefines it as "elevate the elephants." The idea is to focus on (elevate) the biggest, most important opportunities (the elephants) and ignore smaller, less important activities. The concept applies to any business or organization and can deliver outstanding results, if properly pursued.

Pareto was an Italian economist and sociologist. He provided evidence showing that a small percent of the population (20%) possessed most of the wealth (80%). Pareto applied this analysis to different countries and time periods. In all cases, he came up with the same conclusion—that wealth and population correlations were predictably unbalanced.

Key Learnings

❑ Accelerate profit growth, reduce waste, and improve competitive advantage by elevating the elephants. Do **more with less**.

❑ Identify, define, and focus on the most important priorities. Stop the bleeding of resources and profits by foolishly chasing after smaller, unproductive activities. Follow the elephant's rule: *focus on the most important; say NO to everything else!*

❑ Successful leadership is about identifying the right choices and leading others to focus on those choices. Before pursuing any significant activity or project **ask the question:** *What is the biggest elephant I can elevate with the least effort to realize the best return on my effort?* To make elevate the elephants more actionable and accountable, add a specific time frame or date when asking the question.

❑ **Customers, products, and services are not equal.** Define what are strategic, good, and no-customers. Define and prioritize product, service, and other relevant elephant opportunities across the company. After identifying and defining potential opportunities, conduct factual analysis. If supported by ROI, then implement accordingly. Refocus the **best resources on the best prospects.** Carefully let go no-products or no-services (products and services considered for elimination).

❑ Use **Yes, No, & Gray Zones** to identify, set, and refine priorities. The Yes Zone represents the highest priorities. The No Zone denotes the lowest priorities. The Gray Zone symbolizes fuzzy, uncertain priorities. Use data and analysis to continually work towards eliminating the Gray Zone.

❑ Deploy elevate the elephants throughout the company. To be effective, leadership must lead, support, and embrace elevate the elephants. They must **culturally adjust** the mindset of the organization. Proper training is essential. Use competent resources and experts.

TREASURE

6

PACE THE GROWTH

Fear makes Elizabeth clutch the leather reins she holds in her hands. She is grasping them so tightly she might lose control. As she awakens in her dream-journey, Elizabeth feels soreness all over her body. It's been years since she has ridden a horse, let alone one moving at a full gallop.

Elizabeth attempts to get her bearings. She has no idea where she is. There are no roads, no fences, no paths, no borders. There are no obstacles other than her ability to hold on and keep pace.

Elizabeth yells to Joseph, who is riding alongside her, "Where are we?" She calls out again. It is useless. Joseph can't hear above the sound of hundreds of horses and riders producing a high tempo sound of determination. When they finally make a quick stop to change and refresh horses, Elizabeth learns about their dream-journey for Treasure 6.

Fast-Paced Dreams

Elizabeth and Joseph have traveled back in time over eight hundred years to Mongolia. The year is 1204 A.D. They are with Genghis Khan and his warriors. The fast-moving army is concluding an aggressive drive across the plains. Khan is attempting to get in better position before confronting the enemy.

The horses are lightly packed—anything to increase speed. All heavy items are being transported by a well-organized caravan of backup supplies, weapons, and food. Oxen, cattle, camels, and yaks are doing the heavy lifting.

Elizabeth, Joseph, and Khan's army are riding West, towards the Altai Mountains. Unsettled dust obscures their advance. But their focus is clear. It is the eve of an important battle against the Naiman tribe. Jamugha, the formidable leader of the Naiman army, is Genghis Khan's archenemy. He is Khan's blood brother. Genghis Kahn is seeking to avenge a devastating loss to Jamugha several years prior. Time for payback.

More Fires Than Stars

Darkness approaches as they arrive near the foothills of Mount Khangkharkhan. Elizabeth and Joseph have traveled nearly fifty miles in a single day. She contemplates this amazing feat with Joseph. "It is unbelievable when you consider that Khan has moved this entire army, the supplies, and everything needed for battle against the Naiman tribe."

Elizabeth and Joseph overhear Genghis Khan speak to his army. "This will be a great battle. This will be a decisive one. We may lose everything, or we may lose only a few. We must set out against the Naiman in strictest order...we'll march in close ranks like a thorny shrub. Then advancing in lake array, we'll spread out like the waters filling the steppe. Finally charging at the center of their army, we'll drive through their lines like a chisel through wood." Khan then holds up a fistful of arrows and proclaims, "One arrow alone can be easily broken but many arrows are indestructible."

As they are setting up camp, Elizabeth wonders what the men are doing. They are pitching their tents far apart. Each man is building and lighting five campfires. This is many more than needed for heat and cooking. But Khan has a different purpose for the campfires. They are carefully positioned around the outside perimeter of the camp. Joseph explains. "The extra campfires are lit to disguise the size of the army." He elaborates, "Khan knows the enemy will be watching. He wants to bolster the impression of his force." Joseph adds, "To be historically accurate, according to the enemy scout report as revealed in the Secret History of the Mongols, 'Our sentries say, they have more fires than stars in the sky.'"

Despite unfamiliar surroundings and the day's drama, Elizabeth is calm. She is in full learning mode. Joseph uses the time to teach. He asks Elizabeth about their day. "What have you learned from our fast paced adventure?" Elizabeth hits the nail on the head with her reply. "Speed can contribute to competitive advantage." Joseph then asks, "Do you believe Peak Precision Parts' competition is increasing or decreasing its pace?" She quickly replies, "Increasing. A fast pace is becoming the norm." Joseph agrees and makes a point. "Your pace is relative to competition. As such, it's wise to proactively lead the pace of growth. Decide what is the right pace for PPP. Generate your own momentum. Develop specific pace goals. Link them to your dream-statement and TRUE goal."

Limited Life Time

Joseph continues, "To put 'link' into perspective, Khan's dream was to 'unite the whole world in one empire' *during his lifetime*. He was driven to conquer vast amounts of territory as quickly as he could. He devised strategies and tactics to accomplish his dream.

"Let's refer back to business. Peak Precision Parts' Competitive Comparison Question, 'How appropriate is PPP's pace of growth, relative to competition,' scored the sixth lowest and lower than competition. That suggests opportunity to accelerate value creation.

"Many organizations do not pay enough attention to time. It perpetually has a way of slipping away. There are missed deadlines. No one accounts for the X factor, the unknowns. There is lost opportunity. Organizations do not focus on ways to strategically and tactically improve their pace the way Genghis Khan did. What's more, companies sometimes fail to link the growth pace with their dreams and long-term goals. Khan made the connection."

Breakneck Battles

It's blowing hard from the Southwest, the prevailing wind direction. There's a new moon. Joseph and Elizabeth are nestled in a large white felt tent—good material to insulate against cold, wind, and the dark.

Tomorrow's battle will rely on preparation, fortitude, smart tactics, and speed. The evening fades. In their tent, Elizabeth hears men moving, preparing, double checking. They are ensuring everything is in its place. They want to be ready for battle against Jamugha's Naiman army.

At daybreak, a decisive battle is underway. Kahn's riders are taught to ride using only their legs. This provides a competitive advantage. Since they do not have to hold reins, their arms are free to quickly shoot arrows while attacking. As a result, thousands of arrows are unexpectedly heading towards the enemy. This advantage inflicts heavy damage. The battle continues. When the dust clears from the carnage, Khan arises victorious. His planning, tactics, and superior speed are effective. Khan has emerged as the leader of all the Mongol tribes.

In subsequent battles and years, Khan heads East and conquers Beijing, a population of 350,000. Khan continues to learn and advance his strategies and tactics. He presses his pace. Later, Khan's aggressive pursuit of world dominance moves to the West. Persia and Eastern Europe succumb. The city of Baghdad falls in a single attack. For perspective, the Crusaders took over a century to take Baghdad. All told, Genghis Khan's rapid advancement resulted in conquered territory twice as great as the Roman Empire. It was four times the size of Alexander The Great's conquests.

Although inhuman at times, Khan's methods had purpose. They were aligned with his dream of world conquest. He set clear boundaries and expectations. There was little ambiguity. His people and enemies knew the consequences of their choices. For example, his brutal methods of killing the enemy created intense fear. This fear often encouraged enemies to raise the white flag of surrender, without a fight—thereby speeding up Khan's growth pace.

Khan's strategies and tactics were consistent with an aggressive pace. He did not build walls and forts. Instead, he built hundreds of bridges to facilitate swift movement of his armies. Khan moved with breakneck speed. His gait was superior to his competition. Speed was a contributing factor to his success. It was aligned with his dream to rule the world during his lifetime.

Speed Shifts

After enemies were conquered, Khan shifted the pace in the areas that were assimilated. He often took the best attributes from his acquisitions. He leveraged them throughout his empire. Khan transitioned his conquests to a more peaceful society. He did this at a more controlled pace than his speed on the battlefield. To quote Khan, "People conquered on different sides of the lake should be ruled on different sides of the lake."

There was prosperity, running water, civil rules, arts, and culture. In some cases, there was freedom to practice different religions. Khan needed a different pace, so he set a slower one. Joseph says to Elizabeth, "Kahn's adjusting the pace, as appropriate, is a good lesson to apply to businesses and organizations. Re-evaluate and proactively reset your company's pace if goals, gravity-shifts, or circumstances change."

Joseph turns to Elizabeth and asks, "Do you have any initial thoughts regarding improving the pace for Peak Precision Parts?" She responds, "Yes. We must quickly elevate the elephants with our customers and products and find the right innovation leader.

"The medical devices market is growing rapidly. The broad medical parts business is fine but there are more strategic, niche opportunities within. We have always been known for quality manufacturing. As we talked during our second dream-journey (Niche The New), there is a unique need for exceptionally fast and accurate prototype development of medical parts. Because of the urgency to save lives in the medical device world, a rapid speed to market 3-Keys-Strategy is strongly desired by medical device customers — especially those that need mission-critical, complex parts.

"We need to refine our niche and related 3-Keys-Strategy. Elevating the elephants will assist." Joseph responds. "Your instincts make sense. As you know, transitioning to a refined or new niche will not happen overnight. You will likely need to identify different growth rates for the existing business from which you are transitioning and your new niche.

"Another point worth mentioning is that your growth rate will affect your culture. You can feel organizations that have a high growth pace. There is energy. There is quick decision making. There is a bias towards action that is lacking in slower moving organizations."

Slinky-Effect

Joseph offers a pace of growth suggestion for Elizabeth to consider. "You will need to hire more employees as you transition into the accurate and rapid prototyping of complex, mission-critical medical parts niche. Let me share a simple pace improvement opportunity. Clients have realized favorable results.

"Are you familiar with a Slinky?" She replies, "Of course, everyone loves a Slinky." Joseph smiles. He goes on to compare a Slinky (compressed spring toy) to a company's sporadic growth rate. "As you know, a Slinky travels down stairs, end-over-end as it stretches and contracts with the aid of gravity. There are time gaps. There are changes in the rate of motion as the Slinky goes down the stairs—fast, then slow, then fast..."

"As a point of comparison, many higher growth companies follow a similar pattern. They tend to have starts and stops. These delays are often because of short runways in their hiring practices. They hire sales people and hurry to sell. Then they slow down to hire operations personnel to execute on the promises of the sales people. The cycle continues...speed up, slow down. The net effect of this start-and-stop 'Slinky-effect' is that the organization's pace is dramatically lowered. Its growth is impeded."

Elizabeth asks, "What can be done to minimize the Slinky-effect?" Joseph answers, "Plan upfront. Identify all the hires needed. Then identify *earlier time triggers* for finding, hiring, onboarding, and training those positions. Ensure that the budget is aligned with the accelerated time triggers. In addition, the triggers and forecast will likely need to be adjusted as you learn what works and what doesn't work."

Joseph summarizes the benefits of reducing the Slinky-effect. "Smoothing out the Slinky-effect will provide you with more runway to find candidates. The start and stop hiring cycle will be minimized. You will make better hires. Stress will be reduced. Onboarding will be improved. Time gaps will be reduced or eliminated. You will have more control. Net, it will accelerate your pace. It will help you achieve greater success."

Joseph can't help himself. He reprises the old Slinky toy jingle that he frequently heard as a kid. "It's Slinky, it's Slinky, the favorite of girls and boys. Everyone wants a Slinky...everyone, that is, except organizations who want to accelerate their pace." Elizabeth smiles.

Taking Care of Time

Joseph makes another suggestion to improve PPP's growth pace. "An excellent opportunity to improve Peak Precision Parts' speed is to challenge each division, functional area, and team. Inspire them to devise plans and goals focused on improving the pace. Align these 'pace' plans and goals with the dream-statement, 3-Keys-Strategy, and long-term (TRUE) goal. Instill accountability by following up and ensuring everyone is working towards specific pace goals and successes.

"Opportunities to shorten time frames can be applied anywhere. The cumulative effect of improvements in each area will result in accelerating Peak Precision Parts' overall pace.

"Let's take this idea to the individual. Imagine if you asked one of your employees to focus on pace improvements that will speed up their projects by an average of 20%. Do you think this is doable?" She says, "Yes, 20% can be saved by reducing time that is wasted in meetings." Joseph smiles and replies, "Now imagine challenging all 578 of your employees and empowering them with this challenge.

"This seemingly small idea mushrooms into something bigger. What if the pace improvement challenge is stretched to 50% or higher for the most important priorities? Stretch goals challenge the organization to grow at a faster pace. Pacing the growth can lead to a competitive advantage if properly led."

Objectives and Key-Results (OKRs)

Joseph introduces Objectives and Key-Results. "OKRs is a collaborative goal setting and focusing system for individuals, teams, and organizations. OKRs help keep your pace on track. The process is disciplined. It drives a sense of urgency into the company's culture. OKRs were developed by Andy Grove (Intel cofounder and former CEO) and later evangelized by John Doerr (investor in Google, Amazon, Twitter, and other successful startups).

"The first part (the objective), defines *what* you want to achieve in the future. Good objectives are important, concrete, action oriented, and inspirational. Typically, they are achieved within twelve months. However, any timeframe can be used.

"The second part, key-results, define *how* you will achieve the objective. Effective key-results are specific, measurable, and timebound. They are significant outcomes (not activities or trivial tasks) that advance the objective. Typically, there are one to five key-results for each objective.

"OKRs break the long-term into shorter milestones. They keep focus on achieving short-term goals that are aligned with long-term aspirations and goals. I recommend quarterly and yearly timeframes for most OKRs. Take time to think through and define your OKRs. Prioritize your choices (elevate the elephants). Focus on the most important (up to five). Once defined, openly share, track, evaluate, and refine OKRs, as appropriate.

"Here are benefits of an OKR system." Joseph hands Elizabeth a list from the Playbook:

OKR Benefits

○ Growth is kept on track. More can be accomplished in less time.
○ OKRs are an effective tool to focus and align everyone towards the dream-statement and TRUE goal.
○ Accountability is enhanced. Results matter; not unfulfilled promises. A good OKR is crystal clear. It is either achieved or not.
○ Transparency is enhanced. OKRs are openly shared without judgment across the organization.
○ The effectiveness of OKRs has been validated in many organizations (high growth, large, and small).

Elizabeth chimes in, "What about watch outs…downsides?" Joseph replies. "A culture of accountability, trust, and collaboration are prerequisites. OKRs are deceptively simple. An effective OKR system requires an investment in time, resources, training, and leadership. You and your leadership team must all be on board for OKRs to work at PPP. "

Elizabeth says, "OKRs are intriguing. What do you suggest as next steps?" Joseph responds, "First, read Doerr's book, *Measure What Matters*. It provides a good orientation.

"Second, after the leadership team has read the book, start with your top priorities (elevate the elephants). Answering the following question will help define the top OKR choices: *'What are the most important objectives and related key-results over the next three months to move Peak Precision Parts closer to realizing its dream-statement and TRUE goal?'*

"Third, be persistent yet have patience as the leadership team learns what works and what doesn't. Modify and build your own OKR system that meshes with your unique culture. When you gain traction and many of the bugs are ironed out, use the tool to expand it companywide. Have the PPP leadership team come up with specific OKRs to successfully scale an OKR system with *enthusiastic buy-in* at Peak Precision Parts."

As they conclude their Mongolian dream-journey, Joseph shares a quote by Peter Drucker. It captures the importance of taking care of time:

> "Everything requires time. It is the only truly universal condition. All work takes place in time and uses up time. Yet most people take for granted this unique, irreplaceable, and necessary resource. Nothing else, perhaps, distinguishes effective executives as much as their tender loving care of time."

Treasure 6
Pace The Growth

Sage Lesson & Background

Genghis or Chingis Khan (circa 1162-1227 A.D.). Khan demonstrates the importance of establishing a faster pace than competition and adjusting the pace when situations change. If done properly, this often overlooked lesson can be a significant profit accelerator. It can help businesses and organizations become more successful, quicker.

Khan, a Mongol leader and warrior, quickly established one of the largest land empires in history. Within twenty-five years, Khan subjugated more land and people than the Romans did in 400 years. Khan conquered territory comprising more than twelve million square miles.

Key Learnings

❑ Generate momentum. **Proactively lead the pace of growth** to achieve a competitive advantage, accelerate profit, and realize more potential. Set pace goals. Ensure strategies and tactics support the growth rate. Align growth with the TRUE (Tied-to-profit; Risk-aligned; Unmistakable; Explosive) goal and dream-statement.

❑ **Avoid Slinky-effects.** Identify future hires and establish *earlier time triggers* for important positions. Align these new time triggers with the budget and forecast.

❑ Challenge each functional area, team, and individual to **set specific goals to improve the pace**. Consider pace improvements that speed up projects by 20% or faster.

❑ **Vary the pace based on circumstances**. Different areas can have different growth rates. Evolve and adjust the pace as material circumstances change. **Shift speed** to adjust to gravity-shifts, competitive dynamics, available resources, and other relevant factors.

❑ **Take care of time. Leverage OKRs** (Objectives and Key-Results) to drive a sense of urgency and accountability into the company's culture. OKRs help the organization achieve more in less time and effectively keep the pace of growth on track.

TREASURE

7

A UNIQUE POSITION:
A BETTER DECISION

Warm light illuminates the countryside. Elizabeth hears the soothing sounds of the Arno river in the distance. It meanders through soft-edged valleys. A cobalt blue sky breathes splashes of reflected light off the river's surface. Green hillsides are speckled with slowly grazing sheep. Elizabeth and Joseph appreciate the tranquil scenery.

They have traveled back in time to a small Tuscan village near Florence, Italy. The year is 1301 A.D. Elizabeth can smell crispness in the air. It reminds her of early autumn days back home. However, the setting is unlike anything in Indiana.

They walk a path that leads to an ancient, post-card village. In the center is a group of villas and a church. The townspeople are watching an artist at work standing near the church. Giotto di Bondone is painting in the shade—a gift of nature from imposing cypress trees. Giotto has assembled a series of robed figures. He is making preparatory studies. Elizabeth and Joseph notice Giotto paying careful attention to the *position* of the models. He accurately captures their perspectives in his sketches.

Seeing is Believing

Elizabeth asks Joseph about Giotto. "I am not familiar with this artist." Joseph replies, "Giotto was an Italian artist. He was a child prodigy. Legend has it that when the Pope's messenger arrived at Giotto's house to request proof of his genius, Giotto promptly drew a perfect circle — in one stroke. The messenger brought the flawless circle back to the Pope as evidence.

"Giotto liberated painting from its Medieval flatness. He influenced later advancements by Renaissance greats, including Michelangelo. This is evident in Michelangelo's work on the Sistine Chapel ceiling.

"On this dream-journey, we are going to talk about important ways to communicate Peak Precision Parts' unique value to current and potential customers. Giotto will be our sage for this topic. Giotto reinforces the importance of going directly to the customer for truth and to *uniquely position* value relative to competitive choices."

That evening, Elizabeth and Joseph walk to the top of a nearby hill. They find Giotto. He is carefully observing the heavens. There are 4,500 pinholes of light attempting to pierce the night sky, each vying for Giotto's attention. He is fixated on one unusually bright star. Elizabeth and Joseph watch Giotto as he makes a sketch of this special light.

Elizabeth and Joseph dream-journey ahead three years. They are in Padua, Italy (forty kilometers West of Venice). The year is 1304. They are inside the Arena Chapel. Giotto is diligently working on the *Adoration of the Magi*. It is one of thirty-seven frescos (paintings on plaster) he is creating in three rows. The Adoration of the Magi is in the middle tier, along the South wall of the Chapel.

Star Bright, Star Right

Just above the freshly painted manger that shelters Jesus, Mary, and Joseph, Giotto is applying gold, orange, and yellow pigments of motion. He frequently refers to his sketch of a bright star. He faithfully depicts the Star of Bethlehem.

Next, they watch Giotto brush ultramarine blue paint around the special star. Dark blue now frames the fiery Star of Bethlehem in the heavens. The complementary colors add more vibrancy, more life. This is the first time an artist has accurately depicted the Star of Bethlehem as a comet. Today, we know it as Halley's Comet.

Joseph makes a connection for Elizabeth. "This is the bright star we observed Giotto sketching three years earlier. This shows the keen powers of observation that Giotto possessed. He went to nature and observed truth. He wanted to paint a star like no other. He wanted to paint it right."

Voyage Into a Sacred Harbor

Elizabeth and Joseph travel forward in time eleven months. They remain in Padua, Italy. The date is March 25, 1305. It's the Feast of the Annunciation. In addition to the religious holiday, all families of the town are celebrating the unveiling of Giotto's finished work. As they enter the Chapel, they overhear Giotto comment to Enrico degli Scrovegni. "Every painting is a voyage into a sacred harbor." Elizabeth and Joseph walk around. They appreciate Giotto's comment. They are in awe.

Giotto is visually telling a story with his frescos. The overall theme is salvation. He has meticulously depicted the life and events of the Virgin Mary and Jesus Christ. There are thirty-seven scenes majestically arranged around the perimeter walls. There are many figures depicted in the scenes.

All gestures, facial expressions, and emotions are based on Giotto's close observations. Clothing has convincing form. It hangs naturally and lifelike on the various religious figures which face inward. They appear emotionally and physically present. Their sides are towards the observer. This creates depth. It adds interest.

Unlike the Medieval styles that preceded Giotto, his frescos are fresh, emotional, natural. There is a real sense of space. The figures are uniquely *positioned*. They are three-dimensional. They are remarkable. They are believable.

Giotto pioneered a more realistic visual language. His accuracy and attention to perspective separated his work from his contemporaries. The Arena Chapel is Giotto's magnum opus.

Truthful Positions

Joseph explains to Elizabeth the reasons he took her to see Giotto. "He was selected as the sage for this Treasure for two reasons. He was among the first to create fresher, more accurate and truthful paintings.

"The second reason is because Giotto *uniquely positioned* his images. He did this better than other artists by using a more three-dimensional effect. This resulted in more lifelike renderings of his subjects.

"Giotto leveraged truth and unique positioning to create better paintings than his contemporaries."

Elizabeth asks Joseph, "How are these two concepts, truth and unique position, relevant to Peak Precision Parts?" He responds, "The short answer is that better understanding customer truths and learning how to uniquely position them will help Peak Precision Parts sell more products. A unique position helps you communicate your offerings in a way that customers can easily see the relative value choices."

Joseph elaborates. "Let's go to the long answer. Peak Precision Parts' customers have a perception of value. It is based on everything they experience before, during, and after the sale. All customer touchpoints shape customer perceptions. Some are rational. Some are emotional. Some are misperceptions of facts. The important thing is to understand how each strategic customer perceives Peak Precision Parts, regardless if they are factually correct or not.

"We will review insights about customer perceptions (including misperceptions of facts). After our lesson about customer perceptions, we will explore the real battleground—where all business games are played. We will conclude this dream-journey by discussing the unique value position. This will help Peak Precision Parts better connect with customers, so they make a better decision—to buy from you instead of the competition."

Changing Perceptions

On the return trip home from their dream-journey to see Giotto, Joseph makes a statement. "Accurately understanding customer perceptions (and factual misperceptions) is essential. The saying that *perception equals reality* (truth) is a good one." To illustrate his point, Joseph shares three examples of misperceptions.

Elephant Perceptions

"The first example of misperceptions is a story of five blind individuals who have never encountered an elephant. Each blind person touches a different part of the elephant and only one part. The first person who feels the trunk says, '*It's a big snake.*' The second person who touches the leg says, '*It's a tree trunk.*' The third person who touches the tusk says, '*It's a large spear.*' The fourth person who touches the side says, '*It's a leather wall.*' The last person who feels the end of the tail says, '*It's a furry mouse.*'

"In this story, the five blind individuals disagree as to what an elephant factually is. That's not the point. The moral of this story is that personal biases and partial experiences shape our perceptions—they become truth to us."

Joseph continues, "When it comes to understanding customer perceptions to set your unique value position, we must take off our blind-folds. We must get out and talk to the source—customers. That is where you will discover truth. The only thing that matters is their perceptions, regardless if they are factually correct or not."

Monopoly Perceptions

For the second example of misperceptions, Joseph reminds Elizabeth of their first meeting when he asked her the '*how you win Monopoly*' question. She excitedly responds, "Pursue the orange monopoly and build three houses on each property." Smiling, Joseph says, "Good listening and recall...I have asked many people, the '*how you win Monopoly*' question. The majority choose the blue properties. This broadly held misperception is reality to them (recall, perception = reality or truth). As you and I know, the orange monopoly is factually better. However, if your customer perceives blue to be better, that is the truth to them—blue is better."

Lincoln Perceptions

Joseph shares a final example about misperceptions. "Virtually everyone who walks by a 1943D copper Lincoln penny on the sidewalk would perceive its worth to be almost nothing. Most would not bother to pick it up. They wouldn't make time to look at the date and mintmark. Without close inspection, the misperception is that it's just another penny—worth one cent.

"It's a very rare Lincoln coin. It was mistakenly struck in 1943 at the Denver Mint in bronze rather than zinc-coated steel. Steel was used that year to conserve copper for World War II. In 2010, that penny sold for $1.7 million. Perceptions of value can vary from facts."

Joseph refers to Giotto. "Do not use internal assessments of customer value. Go externally to the source—current and potential strategic customers. Giotto went to the source. As we observed in the early fourteenth century on that Tuscan hilltop at night, Giotto studied nature at the source. He painted a more accurate Star of Bethlehem. In the village on the outskirts of Florence, he studied and observed figures in robes. Going to the source helped him paint more accurate figures. Giotto sought truth by changing the way he looked at things. In business, changing the way we position things by uncovering customer truth is important."

Perceptions Change

Elizabeth asks Joseph, "What about perceptions that change over time? Many of Peak Precision Parts' customers now seem obsessed with price. Some of our customers no longer appreciate the high-quality manufacturing that we provide. It wasn't always this way."

Joseph responds, "Excellent question. As we learned with Treasure 2 (Niche The New), everyone faces gravity-shifts. Companies, organizations, and even rock-and-roll bands that endure, have a knack for continually understanding changing customer perceptions of value. They do this better than their competition.

"They learn what the customer is thinking and feeling...now. They develop reliable processes to continue to understand changing customer needs and perceptions. They capture the right information and create a unified, more accurate understanding of the customer. They use this information to make strategic adjustments—to pivot.

"Peak Precision Parts is suffering. This is due in part because it did not keep pace with changing customer perceptions. It did not adjust its strategy to those new perceptions (reality).

"If Peak Precision Parts had a reliable, ongoing process to track customer perceptions (the truth), it could have adjusted its niche and strategy years ago. It would be in a better competitive and financial position today.

"Learn from Giotto. Reach out to customers and seek the truth. Work towards a complete end-to-end understanding of strategic customer perceptions—before, during, and after the sale.

"Put strategic customers at the center. View everything from their perspective, not PPP's. Use their language internally.

"Organizations that look inward or rely on customer hearsay or innuendo are more likely to come up with wrong conclusions, which lead to wrong strategies and the wrong value position. Develop the right processes to update changing perceptions."

Elizabeth asks Joseph, "What suggestions do you have to keep abreast of changing customer perceptions?" Joseph responds, "There are many ways to actively, regularly, and comprehensively listen to your strategic customers. Here are a range of approaches to consider for direct and B2B (Business-to-Business) customers."

Joseph shares a list of listening methods from the Strategic Playbook:

Direct-to-Customer Listening Methods

- Observing and listening at every customer touchpoint within your company.
- Directly talking to customers at regular intervals. Face-to-face is one of the best ways to glean emotional insights and rational thoughts that drive customer behaviors.
- Visiting customers at locations where they congregate, shop, and live.
- Listening to customer inquiries and complaints.
- Formal and informal one-on-one and focus group research.
- Voice of the Customer research (ensure the research is accurate, timely, and actionable).
- Digitally enabled listening and research tools (online surveys, online focus groups, social media sentiment analysis, mobile ethnography research...).
- Any reliable and ethical methods that can track customer preferences and gravity-shifts (trends).
- Data analytics that ethically capture, sort, and analyze customer preferences, needs, decision making processes, purchases, and the like.
- Websites and any other internet or social media sites on which customers are communicating.
- Product and service reviews by customers.
- Expert product and service reviews in publications and on websites.

Business-to-Business (B2B) Listening Methods

- Many of the direct-to-customer listening techniques apply to B2B customers.
- Sales calls. Customer relationship management and other customer databases should capture satisfaction (versus other choices), needs (existing and unmet), preferences (in priority order), and what customers are thinking and feeling about you and the competition.

- o Industry conferences, conventions, and trade associations.
- o Strategic business reviews with B2B customers.
- o Talking to employees who have left B2B customers (who are not obligated by non-disclosure or non-compete agreements).
- o Third-party resources who may have knowledge of customer needs, insights, and desires.
- o Stock reports by analysts for publicly traded customers.
- o Customer websites, blogs, and social media sites that customers are communicating on.
- o Tracking and reviewing customer advertising, PR, promotion, media coverage, job postings…

Joseph continues, "Capture the knowledge gleaned by customer listening. Cleanse the information to ensure it is accurate, truthful, useful, and private. Keep it in a safe, central repository. Share it with those who are strategically involved with the customer. Have as comprehensive and accurate an understanding of the Peak Precision Parts strategic customer as possible."

Elizabeth states, "This is very helpful. Thank you. Going forward, Peak Precision Parts will seek customer truth externally. We will develop more accurate and complete listening methods. We will see, hear, and feel the whole truth from the strategic customers' perspective."

Joseph responds, "Terrific. Use customer truth to refine your 3-Keys-Strategy. Sales can use it to refine strategic customer prospecting. Operations can use it to improve the value chain. Marketing can use it to uniquely position your products and services. We will talk about *positioning* in a minute. First, let's talk about the Peak Precision Parts' battleground."

The Real Battleground

Joseph asks Elizabeth where Peak Precision Parts competes. She responds, "All of our customers are in the United States. With that said, in the past five years, we do have significant price competition from China and other offshore countries. So, I would say we compete internationally."

Joseph responds, "The competitive battleground is not in a market, geography, distribution, media, or other channel. The real battleground is the same for every business in the world." Joseph pauses and observes Elizabeth's perplexed reaction. He continues, "Here's an important point: *your battleground is in the hearts and minds of customers...the only place to find truth and win.*

"If potential customers are not aware of you, you are not in the game. If they perceive your value to be equal to other products (services), it will be up to the dice. You will win some and lose some. On the other hand, if you are uniquely positioned and offer more relative value, you will outperform your competition and win more often than you lose."

Position Is Better Than *Proposition*

Joseph discusses the importance of positioning. "When you change the way you look at things, the things you look at change. Let's go back to Giotto. He did not position his figures as static statues with limited dimension. He went to the source. He painted truth. This helped Giotto to place figures in his frescos with their backs and sides towards the audience. He portrayed his figures as multi-dimensional. They were more real. They were more believable. We take this for granted today. Giotto's approach was a dramatic breakthrough in the fourteenth century."

Joseph continues his thoughts. "Many businesses talk about a unique value *proposition*. Proposition is the wrong word. A unique value proposition is like the Medieval artists that painted flat figures before Giotto came onto the scene. They did not have dimension. They did not have accurate perspective. They were not very convincing. They were inferior to Giotto's figures and frescos.

"*Position* is a better word...*position* versus competitive choices. This helps customers decide to choose you over the competition. You want to *frame or position* your offer relative to other choices. Simply put, positioning is a relative game. Concisely and persuasively answer why the customer will buy from you instead of competitive choices. Be crystal clear as to how you want the customer to think about your products and services versus their other choices."

Weave The Unique Value Position Into Innovation & Design

"Ensure your unique value position is consistent with Peak Precision Parts' 3-Keys-Strategy. Directly link innovation with product and service design. This will help drive your competitive advantage.

"Design should not solely be about how the product, service, packaging, or communication materials look. Nor should it be isolated to visual aesthetics. Design should be a comprehensive, synthesizing, strategic communication of the product's or service's unique value position. It starts and ends with the customer experience. It affects everything the consumer experiences before, during, and after the purchase. This includes any perception whether communicated on the internet, in person, or by the product aesthetics and functionality. Recall how well the iPod communicated its unique value position in the Niche The New dream-journey."

All In (100%)

Joseph wraps up Treasure 7 with two questions. First, he asks Elizabeth: "What percent of the 578 Peak Precision Parts employees know your unique value position?"

She responds, "We do not have a well thought out unique value position yet, but we will. With that said, many employees have a reasonably good idea of what our products are. However, most would not strategically position the products."

Joseph asks his second question: "What percentage of Peak Precision Parts' employees are actively and strategically shaping customer perceptions of your unique value position?"

Elizabeth replies, "That percentage would be lower....maybe 20% of our employees are actively and strategically shaping customer perceptions of our value."

Joseph explains why he asked the two questions. "Imagine if 100% of your competitors' employees knew their unique value position and properly communicated it to every existing and potential customer that they had contact with 100% of the time?" She answers, "That would not be good."

Joseph continues, "The good news is that few companies are asking, much less answering, these two questions." Elizabeth comments, "I will teach this to the leadership team. Everyone in the company will be focused on customer truths: not just sales, customer service, or management. The leadership team will better define our unique value position and ensure it is thoroughly understood by everyone in the company. We will be all in— 100%. The entire organization will be focused on shaping our unique value position."

Treasure 7
A Unique Position:
A Better Decision

Sage Lesson & Background

Giotto di Bondone (circa 1267-1337 A.D.). Giotto reinforces the necessity of going directly to the customer for truth and to *uniquely position* value relative to competitive choices. Properly positioned products and services accelerate profits. Additional profit means more potential for positive outcomes.

Giotto, a pre-Renaissance Italian artist, is known as the Father of the early Renaissance. He was devoted to physical and emotional accuracy in portraying figures. His masterpiece is the interior of the Scrovegni Chapel (often called the Arena Chapel or the Chapel of Annunciation). The chapel is located in Padua, Italy. Giotto's frescos have been superbly restored. They are available for viewing.

Key Learnings

❑ To improve sales and profits, **uniquely position your offerings** to customers in a way they can more easily see value choices. You want to be crystal clear as to how you want the customer to think about your products and services versus their other choices. The unique value position concisely and persuasively answers why the customer will buy from you instead of competition.

❑ A unique value *position* **is more effective** than a unique value *proposition*.

❑ **The competitive battleground is in the hearts and minds of existing and potential customers**, the only place to find truth and win. **Go to the source — the customer** — to find the truth. Do not rely on internal company assessments.

❑ Customers have a perception of value based on everything experienced before, during, and after the sale. **All customer touchpoints shape customer perceptions of value**. Have **100% of employees** know and proactively shape positive perceptions of your unique value position at every customer touch point.

❑ Customer value **perceptions change**. Develop the right processes to update changing customer perceptions. Understand customer perceptions (and factual misperceptions) from their viewpoint. **Actively and regularly listen** to customers. Capture and share customer knowledge and insights with those who are strategically involved with the customer.

❑ **Link** the unique value position to the 3-Keys-Strategy and to product and service design.

TREASURE

8

CULTIVATE A HEALTHY CULTURE

Elizabeth and Joseph find themselves among thirty-five women journalists assembled in a small crowded room within the large white house located at 1600 Pennsylvania Avenue.

Joseph and Elizabeth hear a woman begin to speak. "The reason that I am glad to see you all is that I think in the first place it is much more convenient for you to come at the same time and in the second place it saves me time. I imagine there will be times when various ones will ask for special interviews and I will try to grant them.

"It will save my time enormously if I see you all together once a week and do not have to see three now and three later and so on. I feel that your position as I look upon it is to try to tell the women throughout the county what you think they should know. That, after all, is a newspaper woman's job, to form a general attitude of mind and thought. Your job is an important one, and if you want to see me once a week, I feel I should be willing to see you, and anything that I can do through you toward this end I am willing to do."

Eleanor Roosevelt continues to explain why she has convened the first press conference given by a First Lady. "The idea largely is to make an understanding between the White House and the general public. You are the interpreters to the women of the country as to what goes on politically in the legislative national life and also what the social and personal life is at the White House."

First Press Conference by a First Lady: March 6, 1933

Giving Voice to Values

At the conclusion of the press conference, Elizabeth approaches Eleanor and asks, "What contributed to your strength to lead?" In her reply, Eleanor refers to her experiences working for the American Red Cross during WWI to improve hospital care. "I learned about heroism in human nature and its accompanying frailties. Out of my contacts with human beings, I became a more tolerant person. I gained a certain assurance as to my ability to run things and the knowledge that there is joy in accomplishing a good job. I knew more about the human heart, which had been somewhat veiled in mystery up till now. I learned this. And when the War ended, the feeling of relief and thankfulness was beyond description."

Elizabeth thanks Eleanor and asks, "What circumstances influenced your passion to help the less fortunate?" Eleanor refers to an experience when she was eighteen years old.

She taught impoverished immigrant children at the Settlement House on Rivingston Street (New York).

"This was my first introduction to conditions of labor. I had never known anything about conditions of a sweat shop or how the things were made which you saw in the shops. I was being educated. And I saw little children who worked hours on end until they fell off the benches...this was all completely new to me. This was my introduction to labor, labor conditions. So, I was curious about everything. And that's how you took everything that came along, everything you had a chance to do. But I had no fear."

Elizabeth asks Eleanor a final question. "What is your opinion of women in politics?" Eleanor responds, "That there is a place for women in politics I am absolutely convinced. But politics is a comparatively new field for women and for their own good as well as for the women who will come after them, to say nothing of the community at large, they should keep out of office until they are confident they can hold it with ability and personal integrity. And when I say personal integrity, I mean more than dollars-and-cents honesty. I mean the consistent loyalty to an intelligent idea of service which does not allow itself to be swayed by what other people in office might call politic or expedient."

As they depart, Elizabeth embraces Eleanor. She thanks Eleanor for sharing her insights. Eleanor responds with a final thought, "To mature you have to realize what you value most."

After the press conference, Joseph provides a brief background on Eleanor Roosevelt. "Eleanor Roosevelt faced adversity. She had a challenging life. Her mother died when she was eight. Shortly after, one of her brothers died. Her alcoholic father (Teddy Roosevelt's younger brother) died several years after her mother. Eleanor married FDR at age twenty. Afterwards, she had to contend with a controlling mother in-law and a husband who cheated on her. The Roosevelts' lost one of their six children as an infant. To add to the family's sorrows, FDR contracted Polio.

"Eleanor created the servant leadership role and responsibilities of the First Lady. She was a pioneer in communicating with the public. She spoke on a weekly radio program and wrote *My Day*, a syndicated newspaper column. She gave many press conferences, personal appearances, and speeches.

"Eleanor often communicated her personal values and political desires during these media connections with the public. In her words, she wanted 'to do things on my own, to use my own mind and abilities for my own aims.'

"Eleanor Roosevelt reached out to the source (the customer) to hear truth. In 1933, she made this request: 'I want you to write to me…do not hesitate to write to me, even if your views clash with what you believe to be my views.'"

Joseph continues, "She encouraged a free exchange of ideas and discussion of problems. That would be the best way to help her 'learn of experiences which may be helpful to others.' Her request was heard. By January 1934, 300,000 Americans had reached out to her."

Land of the Free

Elizabeth and Joseph dream-journey ahead in time to 1939. They are still in Washington D.C. It is a cold Easter Sunday. They are back on the steps of the Lincoln Memorial. An African American opera singer, Marian Anderson, is leading tens of thousands in the singing of the national anthem of the United States of America.

Joseph and Elizabeth join in singing "The Star-Spangled Banner." "O'er the land of the free, and the home of the brave..." The collective voices of thousands of attendees resonate down the Washington Mall.

Marian Anderson was originally planning to sing at Constitution Hall instead of the Lincoln Memorial. However, the Daughters of American Revolution (DAR) owned Constitution Hall. Sadly, the president of DAR would not allow an African American to sing there. Eleanor was a member of DAR. She wrote to the President of DAR with these words: "I am in complete disagreement with the attitude taken in refusing Constitution Hall to a great artist...you had the opportunity to lead in an enlightened way." Eleanor went a step further than writing a letter communicating her displeasure with DAR. She resigned.

Elizabeth says to Joseph, "Before this dream-journey, I did not know much about Eleanor Roosevelt. I appreciate that she had the courage to be true to her values and what she was passionate about." He replies, "Eleanor was deeply concerned for those who were treated unfairly. She led and turned her values into action. She was persistent. She followed her principles to achieve her dream of establishing fairness and goodness for all citizens of the United States. She took her message to her audience broadly and individually. Eleanor Roosevelt *gave voice to her values.*"

Defining Culture

Joseph continues their journey by stating, "There are three fundamental leadership lessons to embrace from this Treasure. First, a healthy culture is important. If you have an unhealthy culture, it will negatively affect everything in the company. It will reduce the collective value of the Treasures.

"Second, ensure culture is intentionally strategic. When you create a culture and values that are similar to competition, you miss an important opportunity to set your company apart from others.

"Culture is an underutilized way to differentiate your company. It determines what level of talent you bring on the team. It impacts what innovations you create. It affects how employees shape the customer value perception. Culture can materially contribute to building a sustainable competitive advantage.

"A distinct culture builds a more sustainable advantage than a 'me-too' culture. A benefit I particularly like is that a culturally unique organization is difficult for competitors to emulate." Elizabeth asks, "Why?" Joseph responds, "Copying is minimized because competition does not directly see the value of your culture. They can reverse engineer your products and services. It is harder to do this with culture.

"The third fundamental lesson to embrace from this Treasure is that culture is most powerful when you lead and harness each individual voice (behaviors and actions) behind a collective, unique, and healthy culture. Don't leave your culture to the dice. You do not want an unhealthy, ill conceived, or fragmented culture. You do want a purposeful, strategic, and unified culture.

"Be as intentional about cultivating your culture as you are in developing complex, mission-critical medical parts."

A Definition

Elizabeth responds, "Points well taken. Thank you. Here's a basic question: How do you define culture?" Joseph defines organizational culture and introduces the notion of centric cultures:

"An organization's culture is the collective expression of all the individual voices (observable daily behaviors and actions) within the organization.

"You want to unify and reinforce positive individual behaviors. You want alignment and focus. In other words, you want a *centric culture*."

Centric Cultures

Joseph continues, "Companies that embrace centric cultures have a built-in advantage. Leading everyone in the company around centric cultures can be very beneficial." Elizabeth chimes in, "For example?" Joseph replies, "Centric cultures help align interests. They reduce dysfunction. They improve communication. They minimize a silo mind-set. They make it easier to attract and retain like-valued people. They promote a healthy organization."

He elaborates. "Centric cultures help unleash a deep-seated desire to contribute...a desire to be part of something bigger than yourself...a desire to be on a journey...a desire to achieve something worthwhile.

"We are limited in what we can do as individuals. There is more potential when you align like-valued individuals behind a common culture in pursuit of a focused dream. It is ideal when there is a win-win relationship—when both the individual's unique potential and the organization's unique potential can be mutually pursued and realized."

Nine Lives

Elizabeth asks Joseph, "Any 'right questions' to help define Peak Precision Parts' culture and any examples of centric cultures?" Joseph replies, "Yes. Start by answering: what is the most strategic, effective, and rewarding centric culture to help Peak Precision Parts' realize its dream-statement?"

Joseph continues, "There are many choices for Peak Precision Parts' culture. The Strategic Playbook has a list of nine different centric cultures. Of course, there are more. This sampling gives you an idea of potential options." Joseph hands Elizabeth the list:

Examples of Centric Cultures

1. Winning-Centric
2. Family-Centric
3. Giving-Centric
4. Customer-Centric
5. Employee-Centric
6. Innovation-Centric
7. Sustainability-Centric
8. Inclusion-Centric
9. Technology-Centric

After reviewing the centric cultures list, Elizabeth asks, "Is it possible to combine two or more centric cultures?" Joseph replies, "Yes. For example, Winning-Centric can overlay well with many of the other centric cultures including Family, Customer, Employee, and Innovation-Centric. However, be careful. Do not pursue too many centric cultures. Otherwise, you can dilute the focus of your overall culture."

Joseph provides Elizabeth with information and insights for several of the centric cultures.

Winning-Centric

"Typically, companies that create a culture of winning are successful. Attracting people that want to win can drive growth and success. Winners tend to focus on solving problems and strategy. Winners like to be with other winners. Winners tend to pay attention to and capitalize on gravity-shifts. Winners tend to be accountable for results."

Elizabeth asks Joseph, "How do you define a culture of winning?" He replies, "*Consistently* achieving growth (both top-line revenues and especially bottom-line profits). If an organization achieves ten percent or greater profit and revenue growth for three or more consecutive years, it most likely is winning."

Joseph makes an interesting observation about winning-centric companies. "Most of the companies that are winning-centric have fewer employee morale issues. They have real power in attracting people who perform, move up, and contribute to a brighter future—people who want to be on a winning team. As mentioned, it is possible to combine a winning-centric culture with other centric cultures. However, ensure they reinforce each other and do not confuse or dilute the overall culture."

Family-Centric

"Family businesses are a prominent force in the world of commerce. Many of the largest companies are family owned and controlled. There are hundreds of thousands of mid-sized and smaller companies that are family businesses. Here are pertinent facts:

o   Over 50% of the US Gross Domestic Product (GDP) and employment is generated by family businesses (source, Aileron).
o   In most countries around the world, family businesses generate over 50% of non-government Gross Domestic Product (source, European Family Businesses report).
o   Many Fortune 500 businesses are controlled by founding families. This includes companies such as Walmart, Ford, Mars, News Corp, Comcast, Cargill, Koch Industries, and others.

"Family businesses can foster a sense of connection and identity with owners and their family members. Family businesses tend to have strong cultures. Consider this research finding: a high percentage of family businesses (74%) believe they have a stronger culture and values than non-family firms (source, Conway Family Business Center survey). Family businesses tend to take a long-term view. They balance short-term rewards with multi-generational, long-term sustainability."

Giving-Centric

"There is growing interest in altruistic organizations that want to do more than just earn extra profit. This is particularly true with today's younger workers—Millennials. Finding a niche product or service that can contribute to making the world better can attract a select group of motivated and committed employees. This growing blend of non-profit aspirations with for-profit financials can drive a strong culture. It can enable remarkable dreams."

Valuable Values

After they return to Elizabeth's home, Elizabeth and Joseph identify what they believe were Eleanor Roosevelt's top personal values: fairness; honesty; determination; inclusiveness; courageousness; resourcefulness; teamwork; optimism; and responsibility.

Joseph asks Elizabeth, "Any thoughts?" She responds, "Many of Eleanor Roosevelt's personal values would be excellent values for a company like Peak Precision Parts."

Joseph acknowledges her point. He begins a teaching session on values and their importance in defining and leading culture. "Values contribute to the health of a company. They are building blocks for a uniquely superb culture. Well-chosen values that are passionately lived help build an enduring organization.

"Values are the fundamental principles in which the organization believes. Deeply ingrained values motivate, guide, and drive the right actions. They codify what are acceptable behaviors. Every company has values, even if they are not written. Some are not particularly effective. This is because, in part, they are bland, untrue, or not lived."

Joseph goes on to describe important insights regarding the value creation process. "To achieve your dream-statement, it helps to have clear understanding of your values. It takes time to develop the right values for your culture. Values require reflection and thought. For what does the organization uniquely stand? What is its moral compass? Somewhere along the course of business, it's beneficial to discover and codify what you value. As Eleanor Roosevelt said to you, 'To mature you have to realize what you value most.'"

TEAMS^2 Guidelines

Elizabeth asks Joseph for suggestions as to how to develop and live the right values at Peak Precision Parts. Joseph responds, "The TEAMS^2 guidelines from the Strategic Playbook will help you develop and leverage powerful values at Peak Precision Parts. They strengthen the values. They keep lesser, me-too values from weakening your culture. We will go into detail on each of the ten lettered guidelines (two 'T's,' two 'E's,' and so on). As an overview, you want an organization's values to be:

o **T**alked & **T**ransferred.
o **E**very Day & **E**veryone.
o **A**uthentic & **A**ctionable.
o **M**emorable & **M**easured.
o **S**trategic & **S**acred."

Talked & Transferred

"If values aren't *Talked*, they will have less power in shaping Peak Precision Parts' culture. Just as Eleanor Roosevelt did in her press conferences, radio shows, newspaper columns, and personal appearances, communicate Peak Precision Parts' values in a way that fits your personality. Evangelize them if that is your style. If you are a low-key leader, then live them. Coach Wooden was a great role model of a low-key leader that led and lived through his values. There are many ways to lead. To be successful, you do not have to be charismatic.

"Transparency in communication is important if you want an honest and open culture. Consistency in communication is important so that employees do not fill in information voids with incorrect, unhealthy information. Appropriate repetition in talking the values is prudent."

Elizabeth asks Joseph, "From your experience, where are good opportunities to talk PPP's values?" He responds, "Present your values with your dream-statement. Employee handbooks, recruiting, onboarding, training, and review materials are great places to publish and 'talk' your values. Websites, entries to company buildings, conference and break rooms, newsletters, blogs, emails, or any area where employees congregate and communicate are additional places to consider."

Joseph discusses decisions and values. "When you make important decisions that are based on your values, make a connection back to the values used in making the decision. Company meetings or other forms of company communication are good situations and vehicles to make these connections. Find the right ways and means for you and your company.

"Here's a key point: *One of the most powerful ways to lead and leverage values is to live them.*

"The second 'T' guideline refers to the importance of *Transferring* or handing off the values to all employees (new and existing). Start early—with the recruiting process. As discussed in Tap The Top Talent (Treasure 3), use your values to screen for cultural fit during interviews. You want everyone coming in the door to possess the values of the company. This is analogous to good in, good out (conversely, garbage in, garbage out).

"Companies are well advised to have meaningful on-the-job onboarding and orientation sessions. During those sessions, the company can begin to transfer the values. It can explain their importance, how they are used, the expected behaviors and expectations, and so on. This transference process will telegraph to employees that the company places value in its values."

Every Day & Everyone

"The first 'E' guideline, *Every Day*, is straightforward. Good values are omnipresent. They permeate everything in the organization. They are lived and breathed every day, just like oxygen.

"The second 'E' guideline, *Everyone*, is also straightforward. Values apply to *everyone* in the organization. No one is exempt. Everyone knows them. Everyone lives them. Participation is mandatory."

Elizabeth asks, "What about part time employees?" Joseph responds, "Everyone includes part time employees, independent contractors, and consultants."

"Do we involve everyone at Peak Precision Parts in creating our values?" Joseph gives a surprising answer for someone who likes to engage the customer in the development process. "Do not delegate the development of your values to mid management or involve everyone. They are too important. Their development is leadership's responsibility.

"If you invite everyone in the organization to participate in the development of the values, you may end up with a long, bland list of meaningless mishmashes. Values created by committee are less likely to be unique, strategic, and core.

"The values should not be a laundry list of everyone's pet peeves, desires, or personal principles. It's leadership's responsibility to take significant time to develop, incubate, and cull to the essential values."

Authentic & Actionable

"The first 'A' guideline is *Authentic*. Take time to deeply reflect on and determine insights into what the organization truly values. Values must be genuine and ring true. You do not want fake, shallow, or dishonest values.

"Employees who live the values want the company to abide by them, too. If management falsely portrays values, this will backfire. Not only will potential top talent turn away or existing talent leave, customers may go elsewhere—to a competitor that has more meaningful and authentic values.

"The words and the actions must be aligned. You cannot fake authenticity." Elizabeth asks, "How can you tell if the values are genuine?" Joseph answers, "Watch the behaviors. If there is unity and consistency in actions, the organization probably has authentic values."

Joseph continues with a caution, "Your values are not aspirations; they are actualities. The dream-statement is the right place for aspirations, not the values."

Elizabeth asks, "Should our advertising agency help create our values?" Joseph points out that values are different from brand image. "I recommend that the Peak Precision

Parts' leadership team craft your values with a heavy dose of involvement from you, Elizabeth, the new President. Do not let your agency create or modify your values.

"The second 'A' guideline, *Actionable*, speaks to your values' role in guiding choices and actions in the company. Good values provide a useful guide for making the right choices."

Joseph shares an example from his personal work experience where he had to let go of a top executive. "Timing was difficult. The person had excellent skills. We needed the talent at that critical time. However, the individual's values were in conflict with the company's values. That made it an easier decision. When announced that this person was leaving, everyone knew that integrity mattered."

Joseph shares an appropriate quote by Eleanor Roosevelt:

"In the long run, we shape our lives, and we shape ourselves. The process never ends until we die. And the choices we make are ultimately our own responsibility."

Memorable & Measured

"The first 'M' guideline is *Memorable*. Here are three suggestions (not rules) to help make Peak Precision Parts' values memorable. First, it helps if the values are distinctive, engaging, and concise.

"Second, it's better to have fewer, more powerful values. Carefully choose the most important values. Five is a reasonable target (five is not mandatory). The point is to have fewer, more meaningful values rather than many including some that are meaningless. Having fewer will aid in communication and recall of the values.

"Third, consider an acronym to make it easier to communicate and remember the values. If employees can't recall the values, they have less power. They have less value.

"When creating an acronym, adjust the order of the values if that helps. Use a thesaurus to identify alternative yet appropriate words to fit your acronym. However, *do not force fit an acronym*. If the meaning of any of the values is diluted in the least way, forget the acronym."

Joseph shares two examples of values, one using a PEAKS acronym. "These are shared with you, not with the intention that PEAKS values are correct for Peak Precision Parts. Rather, the examples show how easy it is to remember the values when an appropriate acronym is used. With that understanding as a caveat, which version would employees remember better?" Joseph hands her the two examples from the Playbook:

Peak Precision Parts' Values Example No Acronym:

At Peak Precision Parts, people come first and last. Lasting relationships matter to us. We believe that evil has no place in our company. We always learn, grow, and improve to keep complacency away. We keep our promises. They are sacred to us. Speed counts in every decision we make and every product we create.

Peak Precision Parts' Values Example **PEAKS** Acronym:

- ○ **P**eople come first and last—lasting relationships matter to us.
- ○ **E**vil has no place in our company.
- ○ **A**lways learn, grow, and improve to keep complacency away.

o **K**eep promises — they are sacred to us.
o **S**peed counts in every decision we make and product
we create.

Elizabeth answers, "The acronym is easier to recall."

Joseph switches to the *Measured* guideline. "It's a good
idea to validate if the organization is living the values.
Measure the livability of your values when you conduct
employee surveys to determine the overall health of the
company. If you do not conduct employee surveys, solicit
employee feedback in a simple questionnaire. Consider
asking two questions along the lines of: '*Am I consistently
being true to the company's values,*' and '*is the company
consistently being true to its values?*'"

Strategic & Sacred

"The first 'S' guideline is *Strategic*. Many companies have
similar values. They are not unique, nor are they strategic.

"As mentioned at the beginning of this Treasure, culture is
an important way to lead and differentiate your company. I
recommend that one of the values be a key-value. A key-
value directly supports and reinforces the 3-Keys-Strategy.
In the PEAKS values example, 'Speed counts in every
decision we make and product we create,' is a key-value. It
reinforces the differentiated niche offering of *rapid* found
in PPP's 3-Keys-Strategy. A key-value makes strategy
more robust. It helps drive behaviors that customers
perceive as meaningfully different. This contributes to your
competitive advantage.

"An example of a powerful strategic value under Steve
Jobs' leadership was his 'keep things simple' mantra. Jobs
bred simplicity into Apple's products, advertisements, and
culture. This separated Apple from competition.

"While not as strategic, sometimes uniqueness can be portrayed in how you phrase your values. For example, one of Zappos' values is: 'Create Fun and A Little Weirdness.' They distinctly express more than saying 'we value fun people who are different.'

"The last guideline is *Sacred*. You do not want values that are trendy, fleeting, or politically correct. If you have the right values, they do not change. Values have a long life expectancy. They have staying power. Think fifty years to forever."

Values in Action

Joseph connects values to top talent and customers. "As we learned in Treasure 3 (Tap The Top Talent), the right top talent is important. The right values can help in recruiting and retaining the right talent. Values can also help in attracting customers. Like-minded people like to do business with like-valued people."

Elizabeth asks Joseph, "Do you have an example of how to drive values to specific job expectations and behaviors? I am looking for ideas as to how we can effectively put our values into action."

Joseph replies, "Yes, the Ritz-Carlton Hotel Company does this well. Ritz-Carlton has a Credo, Motto, and Employee Promise. These articulate Ritz-Carlton's service values and expectations. Here they are." Joseph hands Elizabeth a document from the Strategic Playbook:

Ritz-Carlton Hotel Company:
Credo, Motto, & Employee Promise

Credo: The Ritz-Carlton Hotel is a place where the genuine care and comfort of our guests is our highest mission. We pledge to provide the finest personal service and facilities for our guests who will always enjoy a warm, relaxed, yet refined ambience. The Ritz-Carlton experience enlivens the senses, instills well-being, and fulfills even the unexpressed wishes and needs of our guests.

Motto: At The Ritz-Carlton Hotel Company, L.L.C., "We are Ladies and Gentlemen serving Ladies and Gentlemen." This motto exemplifies the anticipatory service provided by all staff members.

The Employee Promise: At The Ritz-Carlton, our Ladies and Gentlemen are the most important resource in our service commitment to our guests. By applying the principles of trust, honesty, respect, integrity, and commitment, we nurture and maximize talent to the benefit of each individual and the company. The Ritz-Carlton fosters a work environment where diversity is valued, quality of life is enhanced, individual aspirations are fulfilled, and The Ritz-Carlton Mystique is strengthened.

Joseph elaborates, "Ritz-Carlton has developed proprietary hiring processes that enable it to more correctly identify, hire, and retain employees that fit their Credo, Motto, and Employee Promise. They have translated these into actionable behaviors that are consistent with their values.

"They set clear expectations for the behaviors of Ritz-Carlton employees. They are unique. They are aligned with actions that separate Ritz-Carlton from competition." Joseph hands Elizabeth another document from the Playbook:

Ritz-Carlton Hotel Company
Three Steps of Service & Service Values

Three Steps Of Service
1. A warm and sincere greeting.
2. Use the guest's name. Anticipation and fulfillment of each guest's needs.
3. Fond farewell. Give a warm good-bye and use the guest's name.

Service Values: I Am Proud To Be Ritz-Carlton
1. I build strong relationships and create Ritz-Carlton guests for life.
2. I am always responsive to the expressed and unexpressed wishes and needs of our guests.
3. I am empowered to create unique, memorable, and personal experiences for our guests.
4. I understand my role in achieving the Key Success Factors, embracing Community Footprints, and creating The Ritz-Carlton Mystique.
5. I continuously seek opportunities to innovate and improve The Ritz-Carlton experience.
6. I own and immediately resolve guest problems.
7. I create a work environment of teamwork and lateral service so that the needs of our guests and each other are met.
8. I have the opportunity to continuously learn and grow.
9. I am involved in the planning of the work that affects me.
10. I am proud of my professional appearance, language, and behavior.
11. I protect the privacy and security of our guests, my fellow employees, and the company's confidential information and assets.
12. I am responsible for uncompromising levels of cleanliness and creating a safe and accident-free environment.

Joseph comments, "Ritz-Carlton conducts a comprehensive cultural orientation before new employees engage with customers. Employees are thoroughly trained. They are certified. The cultural orientation helps ensure that employees will deliver the Ritz-Carlton service steps and service values.

"These service steps set clear expectations. They are intertwined with Ritz-Carlton's values, culture, and strategy. Linking these to actionable behaviors and expectations for employees leverages values beyond just guiding principles. They increase the odds that employees know the strategy and culture. They clearly show how employees can live culture through their daily work habits and actions. They define hiring, work expectations, and accountabilities. They are linked to Ritz-Carlton's unique value position and strengthen its CURVE (Customer Unique and Relative Value Equation)."

The Right Direction

"A healthy culture will move you further to the right (strategic direction), towards a strong CURVE. That's where you want to be. That's where competitive advantage, sustainability, and profitability are all superior to competition. The potential to make a positive difference is greater too.

"Here is a revised CURVE illustration defining the right strategic direction. It now includes top talent, operational discipline, elevate the elephants, pace the growth, and healthy culture." Joseph hands Elizabeth a visual from the Playbook that incorporates the revisions:

Customer Unique and Relative Value Equation (CURVE)

Vague Future
Wrong/No TRUE Goal
Weak Strategy
Unremarkable Talent
Inferior Value Chain
Unfocussed Priorities
Slower Pace
Unhealthy Culture

Right Strategic
Direction

Dream Statement
Aligned TRUE Goal
Strong 3-Keys-Strategy
Right Top Talent
Superior Value Chain
Elevate The Elephants
Faster Pace
Healthy Culture

Weak CURVE =
Competitive Disadvantage
- No Differentiation
- High Relative Costs
- Low Profit
- Less Potential to
  Make a Difference

Strong CURVE =
Competitive Advantage
➤ High Differentiation
➤ Low Relative Costs
➤ High Profit
➤ Greater Potential to
  Make a Difference

The Platinum Standard

Joseph recommends that Peak Precision Parts strives toward The Platinum Standard. He discusses attributes of this "ideal" culture. "It does not happen by chance. It takes proactive leadership and persistence. This is a culture where employees thrive. The efforts can lead to a healthy, truly extraordinary company—a lasting legacy. Here are attributes of organizations with Platinum Standard cultures." Joseph hands Elizabeth the list from the Strategic Playbook:

Attributes of Platinum Standard Cultures

○ The organization is healthy. It makes a meaningful difference in the world and adds value to the communities in which it lives. There is stewardship. The culture and corresponding employee behaviors are led, managed, monitored, and adjusted, if off course. The culture resonates with and is reinforced among all levels of employees. There is unified passion to pursue the dream-statement. Values are consistently and passionately lived throughout the organization. Communication and storytelling reinforce the culture and its values. Communication effectively connects today with tomorrow. It connects personal and organizational values.

o Culture and strategy are intertwined—they mutually support each other. Culture differentiates the company from competition. It builds a sustainable, difficult to copy advantage.

o Customer and other relevant knowledge is shared. Appropriate information is readily available. There is transparency, consistent clarity, and confidentiality.

o There is little self-deception. People succeed based on performance, not politics. Trust, commitment, and accountability are high. Positive behaviors, consistent with the culture, are rewarded and reinforced. Conflict is confronted, not avoided. Attention is paid to achieving collective results.

o Leadership can be from anywhere. Empowerment and decision making processes are clear. They are pushed downward and out to the front-line—where customer perceptions of value are shaped.

o Calculated risk-taking is rewarded. The focus is on solving and preventing problems, not blaming and judging. Failures are seen as opportunities to learn and improve. Successes are celebrated.

o The truth, objective data, and information are used whenever possible. Opinions are only used when objective data is unavailable (or there isn't adequate time to obtain solid facts).

o The organization leverages employee strengths. It does not dwell on weaknesses.

o The company offers favorable benefits and emotional rewards. Pursuit of personal development and growth are rewarded.

o There are the highest levels of professional and personal satisfaction among employees.

Treasure 8
Cultivate A Healthy Culture

Sage Lesson & Background

Anna Eleanor Roosevelt (1884-1962). Eleanor Roosevelt personifies the merits of defining, leading, and cultivating a healthy culture, as well as being true to and voicing your values.

An American First Lady, diplomat, and activist, Eleanor Roosevelt significantly reshaped the role of First Lady. She advocated for civil, worker, and women rights. She led cultural change through her values, words, and actions. She was bestowed with thirty-five honorary degrees including one from Oxford University. Eleanor Roosevelt is regarded as one of the most respected and admired women of the Nineteenth Century.

Key Learnings

❑ Well chosen (defined), lead, and lived cultures activate a healthy and enduring company. An organization's **culture is defined** as: *the collective expression of all the individual voices (observable daily behaviors and actions) within the organization.* A culture is most powerful when you harness each individual voice behind a collective, purposeful, and unique culture.

❑ **Centric cultures** cultivate everything in the company around the culture. They connect and unleash a deep-seated desire to contribute and be part of something bigger than the individual. They make it easier to attract and retain like-valued people and customers.

❑ Values are an important component in shaping a company's culture. They motivate, guide, and drive the right behaviors and actions. **Use TEAMS^2 guidelines to develop and leverage powerful values** (Talked & Transferred; Every Day & Everyone; Authentic & Actionable; Memorable & Measured; and Strategic & Sacred).

❑ Leadership should **intentionally choose a strategic culture**. When you create a culture and values that are similar to competition, you miss an important opportunity to set yourself apart. At least one of the values should directly support and reinforce the 3-Keys-Strategy.

❑ **Translate values into defined actionable steps** that are linked to strategy.

❑ **Strive for The Platinum Standard** (culture) through proactive leadership, effort, and persistence. This is paramount to realizing a healthy, extraordinary, enduring company.

TREASURE

9

MAKE WORK SIMPLE

Joseph and Elizabeth climb three flights of stairs and open the door to a large, irregular art studio. Elizabeth thinks she is walking into a three-dimensional painting. Brilliant white walls complement rich black floors. Rectangular shapes of yellow, blue, gray, and red cardboard are tacked on walls. The carefully positioned easel, wicker chairs, and work tables are warm white. Red, gray, and black pigment the couch, side tables, and a heater. Even the Victrola is painted red. Several gray rugs are placed 90 degrees adjacent to a red rug in the center of the floor.

They are visiting Dutch artist Piet Mondrian. It's October 1930. They are in the 15th Arrondissement, Paris, France. Also present is an American—Alexander Calder. This is Calder's first in a series of meetings with Mondrian. Mondrian's thoughtfully ordered studio is designed to mirror his art. It is a modern, clean, pure room. There is no unnecessary ornamentation. Piet has opened the white curtains of a large window. Sunlight dances on the joyful colors in his studio.

Joseph tells Elizabeth that Treasure 9 is about making the work flow and organizational structure simple. "Making work simple is directly linked to and amplifies Treasure 8 (Cultivate a Healthy Culture). Treasure 9 focuses on how well you leverage and treat your people resources. If you implement simple and fluid work flows, you can improve employee effectiveness and happiness. You can improve the health of the organization."

Joseph discusses why Alexander Calder is the sage for Treasure 9. "Calder saw value in keeping it simple. He did not complicate his artwork with unharmonious colors, confusing shapes, or unrelated ideas. He reduced complexity and pioneered the creation of fluid art in motion (the mobile). Here is a quote by him:

> 'The trouble with a lot of artists today is that they have too much technique and equipment. They don't know what to do with it all. If you cut down on it, you can work more strongly within narrower limits.'"

Joseph continues, "Simple organizational structures and work flows are not easy to accomplish. It requires thinking strategically and experimenting to make work simple.

"Many companies have organizational structures that are complicated and rigid. They slow down the natural flow of work. They restrict and frustrate workers. Do not complicate work. Design work flow and organizational structure to be consistent with your strategy. Keeping things simple will help ensure this linkage occurs."

Joseph provides background on the first stop of their dream-journey. "Calder spent time early in his career mingling with avant-garde artists, including Joan Miro, Fernand Leger, Jean Arp, and Piet Mondrian. Calder discovered breakthrough approaches to his art from these interactions, especially exchanges with Mondrian."

Simple Sparks & Benchmarks

During their visit to Mondrian's studio, Calder sees how Mondrian championed two simple artistic themes: the use of primary colors and the use of rudimentary geometric shapes. Before leaving, Calder suggests to Mondrian, "Perhaps it would be fun to make these rectangles oscillate?" Piet, with a serious countenance, responds, "No, it is not necessary. My painting is already fast."

According to thirty-two-year-old Calder, this first interaction with Mondrian in his Paris studio provided Calder with the spark to pursue abstract art: "This was the shock that started things."

As they descend the stairs of Mondrian's studio, Joseph and Elizabeth start a dialogue. They review what they have learned from their glimpse into a tipping point of Calder's artistic development and the experience of seeing Piet Mondrian's unusual studio. Joseph asks Elizabeth for her reactions. She responds, "It was fun to see Calder's thoughts in motion. He was excited to take the primaries and geometric shapes and turn them into oscillating art.

"I can't believe how exacting Mondrian was. He was totally immersed and focused. Mondrian's studio was a living, 3-D model that reinforced what he felt was important. Everything was about one thing: his art." Joseph encouragingly replies, "Well done…were any ideas sparked about Peak Precision Parts' organizational structure and making work easier to do?"

Elizabeth replies, "Yes. When I think about it, our org-structure seems disconnected. We have too many layers. We make it hard to make decisions. Communication has bottlenecks. It does not flow as easily as it can. The organizational structure is not strategically thought out. It's an afterthought. It's not carefully designed the way Mondrian and Calder thought through their art.

"We need to learn from Mondrian and Calder. We need to strategically design our work structure and flow. The amount of reporting layers can be reduced. We can simplify. We need to make everything centered around achieving our new dream-statement—the way Mondrian centered everything around his art."

Joseph applauds her insight. He goes on to share another point. "Calder was benchmarking. To simplify and make your work easier, you may want to visit a few companies. Benchmark companies that have great organizational structures where work is easy to do. Look at the Baldrige Award winners. They often share their successes and generally are open to benchmarking. Look at high tech companies, too. They tend to move fast."

"Organizations like Peak Precision Parts can quickly improve through benchmarking. You have the benefit of seeing specifically what making work easy to do looks like—much as Calder saw what abstract art, the primary colors, and simple geometric shapes looked like. He was the first to turn them into moving, fluid art."

Joseph adds a caution about benchmarking. "Benchmarking helps you quickly improve, but only up to a point. After that, innovate beyond what you learned—the way Calder applied Mondrian's simple color schemes to moving sculpture."

Simplicity of Form

Elizabeth and Joseph dream-journey to their next destination: New York. Calder has journeyed far in the thirteen years since their visit to Mondrian's Paris studio.

The date is Wednesday, September 29, 1943. They are at the Museum of Modern Art (MOMA) for an exhibition of almost 100 works by Calder. At age forty five, he is the envy of his peers. The Director of the show, James Johnson Sweeney, prepared the following remarks for the Calder MOMA show:

> "He has always avoided modeling in favor of direct handling...such an approach has fostered a simplicity of form and clarity of contour in his work...his sculpture is a kaleidoscope of form and

color in unpredictable constellations. He combines nature with geometry, constructs balances operated by mechanics or wind, and cuts fantastic and beautiful shapes out of air…he is an American able to preserve his national and personal idiosyncrasies in active balance with a dominant respect for form and organization."

They enter Calder's exhibition on the first-floor galleries of MOMA. Elizabeth notices the crowd is comprised mostly of forty year and older adults. When she thinks about it, the lack of young attendees, especially men, makes sense. Most of the young male portion of the Greatest Generation are fighting in Europe and the Pacific.

While walking through the Calder exhibition, Elizabeth and Joseph overhear someone commenting on the show; "It is a welcome and refreshing relief from the daily drama coming from the news reports of the War."

They approach the Sculpture garden. Elizabeth and Joseph listen to a conversation between an art aficionado and Henry McBride (an art critic). McBride states that the exhibition, "Contains an astonishing number of proofs that nature never can be entirely thwarted and that even when at the last gasp, as I presume nature is at the moment, she can still supply to poets and to genuine artists the mana which the soul craves and upon which the soul thrives." The art aficionado succinctly responds, "Yes, great art affirms the positive aspects of life."

Joseph comments to Elizabeth, "And simple organizational structure affirms the positive aspects of work."

Parallel Structures

The first large Calder sculpture Elizabeth and Joseph approach is a six foot plus high stabile. It is made from painted sheet steel, wire, and five painted wood spheres.

It is titled, *Morning Star*. The sculpture was constructed by Calder in 1943:

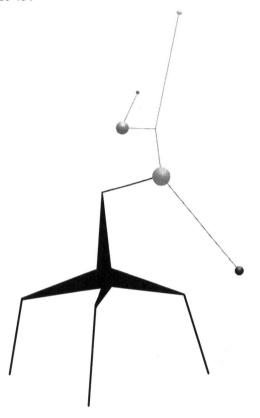

They get into a conversation about the parallels between this artwork and good organizational structure within a company. Joseph starts the conversation. "Calder's use of primary colors and a solid, simple tripod foundation are analogous to having a simple organizational structure (with few reporting layers) so that work is easier to do, and the right decisions are made quicker."

Elizabeth picks up the connections. "The yellow sphere at the top is like the dream-statement—what everyone is working towards. The five planetary spheres are like independent functional areas with constant communication connecting them." After dissecting a few more *Morning Star* analogies, they move onto a larger Calder work.

Elizabeth and Joseph view a nearly nine-foot-high mobile titled, *Red Petals*. It has a large black plant-like metal base that flows upward. At the top of the base is a mobile configuration of eleven elements. These elements are held in the air by gently curved wire tendrils.

Joseph asks Elizabeth, "What do you think?" She replies, "It's a graceful structure. It easily engages. I like the solid, well balanced foundation, an important element of a good organization. I like the simple balance and fluidity of the elements. I like the forms. They are connected. They flow in unison. They communicate a unified, positive impression of life. *Red Petals* is analogous to a simple, fluid org-structure. A structure where information, ideas, decisions, and work easily flow, and the workers enjoy work." Joseph responds with excitement, "Wow, you are really getting this." Elizabeth smiles.

After spending the day admiring and analyzing the Calder exhibition, they depart MOMA. Elizabeth reflects on the importance of this day for Calder. The MOMA exhibit clearly validated Calder's preeminence as a leading American artist. He was the youngest artist so honored at the time.

Roxbury Takeaways

Joseph and Elizabeth's last destination is to Calder's rural studio on Painter Hill Road in Roxbury, Connecticut. It's a clear sunny day in New England. The year is 1972.

The studio has abundant natural light flooding from tall walls of glass paned windows. Even though Calder is seventy-four years old, they hear busy sounds—clanging, scrapping, and hammering. Calder is wearing his favorite red flannel shirt. A pair of pliers protrudes from the back pocket of his baggy trousers. He is bashing away on metal to form simple, artful structures.

Calder's Roxbury studio looks like a workshop, laboratory, and studio all rolled into one large workspace. Partially developed mechanical systems and devices are hanging from the ceiling. Wire, metal, wood, and other materials crowd the perimeter. There is clutter, creativity, and significance everywhere. Elizabeth comments to Joseph, "It's obvious that Calder is interested in experimentation and problem solving." Joseph replies, "Leonardo da Vinci would approve."

Elizabeth looks through a box of sketches from the 1930's. They offer clues that earlier in life Calder "composed simple motions" by precisely measuring and calculating the movement and workings of his mobiles.

Elizabeth's attention drifts. She wonders to herself, "Is this just a dream or is any of it real?" She approaches Calder and asks, "Are we real to you?" In an uplifting, philosophical manner, Calder responds. "If you can't imagine things, you can't make them, and anything you imagine is real."

On their journey home, Joseph asks Elizabeth, "What learnings can you apply to Peak Precision Parts from visiting Calder's studio today?" She says, "His constructive imagination was contagious. I need to foster this attitude at work. His early drawings remind me that it's a good idea to revisit the basics. Calder also continued to experiment. Our organizational structure must be aligned with our basic strategy. This, and experimentation, will help us realize the right structure and work flow."

Bash Away Barriers

Joseph comments, "Good observations. We have seen how masterfully Calder bashed away complexity and used the principles of *simplification* and *fluidity* to create his wonderful mobiles. Calder can teach us a thing or two.

"Poor communication, bureaucracy, dysfunction, unnecessary layers, and silos hinder an organization's health. These barriers get in the way and must be minimized. The negative impact on the organization's health is cumulative. Think like Calder. Bash away these and other obstacles that make work complicated and hard. This diagram from the Strategic Playbook visually captures this idea." Joseph hands it to her:

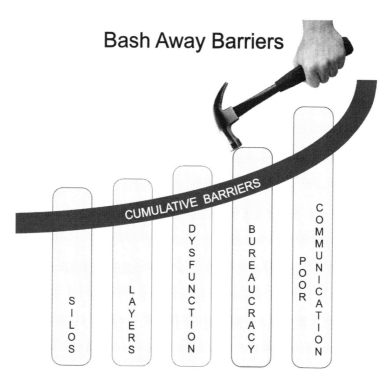

After reviewing the diagram, Elizabeth comments, "We have these barriers in varying levels at Peak Precision Parts." Joseph replies, "So does every company. Let's briefly sort through the barriers and opportunities for simplification identified in the diagram, starting with poor communication."

Poor Communication

"Organizations that are connected through good communication flow are healthier than companies with poor flow. To cultivate a healthy culture and do work well, workers need quick access to the right information. Operating with transparency is important to build trust. Sharing knowledge helps workers be more productive and successful. Proactively think about the best way to ensure there is good communication flow. Remove barriers to fluid communication (except when they are needed for confidentiality and privacy).

"A simple, unrestricted flow of the right communication is critical to improve work flow. It is essential to maximize employee effectiveness and organizational health.

"Provide consistent clarity…in roles, responsibilities, decision making authority (and processes), expectations, boundaries, accountability…the list goes on. The underlying need is similar. Leaders need to clearly and effectively communicate. Consistency in providing clear communication propels leadership and the organization in the right direction. It reduces unnecessary confusion. It bashes away barriers to doing great work."

Bureaucracy

Joseph comments on the second barrier. "Be on the lookout to combat bureaucracy. There is a natural progression towards organizational complexity—making it hard to get the right things done. As an organization grows, there are systems, processes, and policies that need to be added. Carefully select these. Only add ones that truly improve value for customers and employees.

"Elbow out anything that makes work harder to do. Avoid adding complicated systems, rules, processes, and procedures. They can contribute to an unhealthy culture, slow the pace of growth, and choke the joy out of work. As the leader of Peak Precision Parts, fight the natural evolution to add complexity. Avoid inhumane bureaucracy.

"This starts with properly defining and understanding the culture. It continues with clear roles, expectations, responsibilities, and accountabilities. Align individual goals with the TRUE and pace improvement goals."

Dysfunction

Elizabeth comments on dysfunction. "The peer-learning forum I am in just read *The Five Dysfunctions of a Team*, by Patrick Lencioni. Thankfully, we function reasonably well at PPP." Joseph comments, "You are fortunate. Many companies have dysfunction. This is often a root cause of an unhealthy culture.

"Lencioni's book and approach provide excellent solutions. They bash away the barriers of dysfunction. Follow Lencioni's advice to: 1) build vulnerable trust; 2) reduce the fear of conflict; 3) achieve commitment; 4) embrace accountability; and 5) focus on the right collective results."

Layers

Joseph transitions to discussing layers. "Reduce reporting layers to the point that work flows easily. Base the number of reporting layers in part on facilitating quicker, better decisions, and improving responsiveness to customers.

"You want front-line employees to know the broad strategy and principles to guide them in making the right decisions quickly. You want them properly trained to operate in real time. This is much faster than hierarchical organizations that capture information, send it back to management, move it up and then back down the line, and finally out to the front-line.

"Reduce reporting layers but not to the point that bottlenecks occur, or the span of coaching is too wide (managers cannot effectively coach)." Elizabeth asks, "Is there an optimal span of coaching ratio?" Joseph replies, "If you ask ten different managers, you'll get ten different answers. There isn't a magic ratio. It depends on the complexity and nature of the work, the capabilities of the employees, the effectiveness of the coaches, how self-directed the teams are, and the like. Find the optimal tradeoff between a wide span of coaching and having fewer direct reports so that effective coaching and mentoring can occur. Experiment and find what works best for Peak Precision Parts. As we learned from Calder, err on simple."

Silos

Joseph switches the topic to silos, the last barrier identified in the diagram. "Silos (functional, territorial, political, and other perceived boundaries) can slow action, frustrate workers, and negatively affect performance. Eradicate silos that get in the way of doing great work. Ensure the knowledge and skills to deliver desired outcomes reside within cross-functional teams. It's beneficial to have qualified leaders to help define objectives, prioritize work, and take the lead in reducing silo mentalities.

"Have different team members lead depending on their expertise and the situation. Make continual learning and sharing knowledge part of the team's DNA. Have everyone on the team, regardless of functional area (or other perceived boundary), share learnings to improve.

"Design the reward structure to foster accountability and collaboration and to minimize functional turf.

"Setting standards for prompt decision making helps teams perform well across silos. Working to improve decision making (quality and speed) is an ongoing opportunity and responsibility of the team. High functioning teams that ignore silos can dramatically improve organizational health and the odds for success."

Elizabeth asks, "Can you recommend anything to bash away silo confusion and conflict?" Joseph replies, "The RACI Matrix (**R**esponsible, **A**ccountable, **C**onsulted, **I**nformed) is a simple tool that clarifies accountabilities, responsibilities, communications, and roles among team members from different silos. It minimizes confusion on project teams and activates the respective roles. The RACI Matrix (RACI) should be used by cross-functional and self-directed teams that work on important, strategic projects.

"RACI is a structured approach to bash away silo confusion and conflict. It clearly identifies four broad roles. Here are the RACI role descriptions from the Playbook."

- **Responsible (R)** — The doers who actually do the work and complete the tasks and deliverables. Typically, there are multiple R's. However, their specific tasks should be identified. Ensure no team member is overburdened with too many responsibilities.
- **Accountable (A)** — The individual "owner" held accountable for the thorough and correct completion of the task or deliverable. To improve accountability there should be only one A per task. The A must sign off or "approve" the task or work for all R's. As such, this role is sometimes known as the Approver.
- **Consulted (C)** — The subject matter experts whose advice is sought during the project. Only include a few C's — those that can offer the best advice and have the most impact on the project's success. Otherwise, the process can get bogged down by too many unnecessary voices. Communication is typically two-ways with C's.
- **Informed (I)** — This includes anyone that should be updated on the project. The I's are not formally consulted and do not actively participate. Communication is typically from the team to the respective I's.

"There are a number of RACI variations. All typically use a two-dimensional matrix to define and communicate responsibilities and avoid silo friction. Use off the shelf software (Excel, Numbers, Word, PowerPoint) to create the matrix. Here is an example."

RACI Matrix Example

	Lisa	Steve	Markus	Elizabeth
Task A	R	A	C	I
Task B	R/A	R	C	I
Task C	A	C	R	R
Task D	A	R	C	I
Task E	C	A	R	I

R = Responsible, A = Accountable, C = Consulted, I = Informed

"To implement RACI, use these five simple steps." He hands her the five RACI steps from the Strategic Playbook:

1. **Identify High Impact Work Steps** (deliverables). Do this as a team exercise to improve alignment and buy-in.
2. **Determine Key Tasks/Decisions**. These are the important tasks and decisions needed to successfully complete the project.
3. **Define Single Point Accountability**. Ensure every task has only one person responsible—the A.
4. **Collaboratively Build the Matrix**. Do this as a team by listing the tasks (deliverables) and marking each task with one of the four roles. Some tasks may not have C's or I's. However, every task must have one A and at least one R. Start with A's (those accountable) and R's (those responsible for doing the work). Analyze and optimize the matrix to prevent duplication, eliminate unnecessary R's and C's, and ensure all appropriate tasks and roles are identified.

5. **Obtain Feedback to Ensure Buy-In**. Have all R's, A's, and C's sign off on the matrix. Revise the matrix based upon input from participants (except the I's). Update the RACI as the project progresses based upon project progress and learning.

"Here are benefits of the RACI Matrix." Joseph hands her the last RACI document from the Playbook:

o Minimizes silo barriers—friction, frustration, blaming, and work flow malfunctions that sometimes occur when functional boundaries are crossed.
o Clearly identifies expectations among team members. Ensures all team members are appropriately engaged and aligned. Accountability is defined and aligned.
o Improves communication and connects people to tasks and accountabilities.
o Identifies potential duplication of efforts and gaps needed for tasks—before the project start.
o Ensures stakeholders are aware of and agree to what responsibilities they have to the project.
o It is easy to teach and use.
o It has been validated in many organizations.

Elizabeth asks, "What about downsides?" Joseph replies, "There can be friction when obtaining buy-in if there is disagreement on roles and responsibilities. However, it's better to work through this upfront. If there is underlying dysfunction on the team, RACI will not fix it.

"Another RACI downside can occur if someone is too detailed and wants to include every conceivable task in the matrix. Find the right balance of tasks to include based on team and company culture and project complexity. Lastly, don't over use and complicate the tool. Elevate the Elephants—use RACI on the most important, highest-value projects. Use simple in-house software to create and update the matrix."

Simple Questions

Elizabeth asks Joseph, "Do you have any 'right questions' to help with simplification and making work easy to do at Peak Precision Parts?" Joseph responds, "Here is a list from the Strategic Playbook. As a starting point, survey and interview employees to uncover obvious and hidden pockets of complexity that hamper effectiveness and contribute to an unhealthy organization." Elizabeth thanks Joseph as she looks over the list:

o What are the biggest barriers (problems) and corresponding opportunities to improve and simplify work flow throughout the organization?
   ▪ Does the organization waste too much time on internal processes that do not contribute to strengthening the CURVE, building competitive advantage, and delighting strategic customers?
   ▪ What organizational area is the most complicated and important—the prime candidate to simplify in the organization?
o What are the biggest communication bottlenecks within the organization and how can they be improved?
o How much unhealthy bureaucracy is there in the organization?
   ▪ What is the root cause?
   ▪ How can it be minimized and prevented in the future?
o How dysfunctional is the organization?
   ▪ Review Patrick Lencioni's specific questions in his The Five Dysfunctions of a Team book.
o What are the optimal number of reporting levels to accomplish the TRUE goal, dream-statement, and effectively pursue the 3-Keys-Strategy?
   ▪ Is the span of coaching ratio appropriate?
   ▪ Are there overlapping or unclear roles and responsibilities that need to be addressed?
   ▪ Does the organization make effective decisions fast enough to delight strategic customers?

- What specific barriers can be removed to improve the organization's ability to work across real and perceived silos?
- What other cultural barriers diminish the joy of work, hurt work effectiveness, and organizational health?
- How prepared is the organization in terms of resources and training to effectively combat poor communication, bureaucracy, dysfunction, and other barriers that slow down and make work difficult to do?
- What are the most important Make Work Simple OKRs (Objectives and Key Results)?
  - Who is specifically accountable to do what and by when?

Here Comes the Sun

Elizabeth is happy after returning home from their Calder dream-journey. She has a sense of optimism—she can lead a successful turnaround of Peak Precision Parts.

When they enter her family room, Elizabeth reveals to Joseph, "This dream-journey was special. I have always been fond of art, especially of Alexander Calder." She confesses, "This is the first sage with whom I have a personal connection." She elaborates, "I was blessed every day to look at a Calder print. My parents purchased it in 1975 and hung it on the wall in my bedroom. It has been with me for as long as I can remember."

Elizabeth points in the direction of the Calder. It is hanging above her couch. Elizabeth continues metaphorically, "Calder's bright rays have followed me from my childhood home, to school, my first apartment, my starter home, and now they shine here. I didn't realize how meaningful this Calder is to me until today."

Joseph can see that the artwork's unified composition communicates the simple joys of a bright, uplifting, sunny day. It depicts a sun (upper left) with rays reaching across a yellow sky. In the middle, there are three blue horizontally aligned geometric shapes. They suggest an ocean. Below, simply rendered black and white angular lines form mountains. They break the horizon and reach up to the sky. Joseph notices that the focal point, the sun, is red—Calder's favorite color.

Elizabeth's Alexander Calder Print

Unexpected Question

Before departing, Joseph asks an intriguing question. "If you could wave a magic wand and choose someone to visit for our last dream-journey, who would be most meaningful to you?"

Elizabeth gives the unexpected question thought. "These journeys have all been tremendous...the first person that comes to mind is Marie Curie. I learned about her accomplishments in my High School chemistry class. As a woman living in the nineteenth century, she prevailed against the odds. She was very dedicated to her dreams and accomplished much. Marie Curie has been an inspiration to me."

Joseph absorbs what Elizabeth said. He does not respond.

Connected Treasure

After Joseph leaves, Elizabeth draws a conclusion from Treasure 9. "This dream-journey reminds me that the Treasures are interlinked. They work together and support each other. When pursued together, sustained success will be greater." She recalls an illustration in the Strategic Playbook that reinforces her point:

Ten Connected Treasures

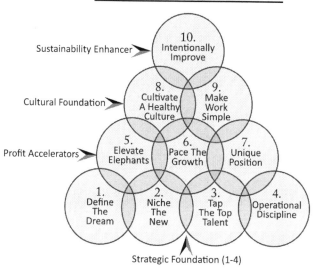

Elizabeth thinks about the diagram. She reminisces over the dream-journeys. "The first four Treasures provide the strategic foundation. Treasure 1 (Define The Dream with Dr. Martin Luther King Jr.) showed the power and importance of providing the overall strategic compass—the dream. Peak Precision Parts defined a great dream-statement that everyone buys into using the Playbook's FATE guidelines (Future dream; Align; Teach strategy; Easy to share).

"We set an excellent TRUE goal (Tied-to-profit; Risk-aligned; Unmistakable; Explosive). It focuses on profit which increases the potential for Peak Precision Parts to prosper, make a difference, and give back more. We determined the right measures to track success along our journey. To improve traction and effectiveness, we engaged all PPP employees to develop and own shorter-term goals aligned with the dream-statement, TRUE goal, strategic dashboard, and annual budgeting processes.

"From Treasure 2 (Niche The New), we have a good start on our 3-Keys-Strategy. This, along with lessons from Steve Jobs, the master spotter (innovator), will strengthen PPP's competitive advantage. We have identified and hired a strong candidate to lead the innovation team—thanks to Joseph's innovation leader role description. As we bring to market successful niche products, we will strive for an absolute advantage, an ideal state where customers do not emotionally or rationally consider other choices.

"Meeting Coach Wooden in Treasure 3 (Tap The Top Talent) was a highlight. He reinforced the importance of preparation, having thorough processes, and setting high standards for the most important ingredient in our company—talent. We have an improved system of finding the right top talent. We now identify and nurture our Stars. We even have a handle on succession. Ironically, poor succession planning is the reason I am at PPP.

"Henry Ford (Treasure 4) personified relentlessly striving for effective utilization of resources to strategically drive down costs. As we continue to get our operational disciplines in order at PPP, we are strengthening our competitive advantage, especially the 'what customers relatively pay' (bottom) part of the CURVE (Customer Unique and Relative Value Equation). I have little doubt that Lisa, our VP of Operations and her team will soon discover *value chain breakthroughs*—new activities that solve old problems in entirely new and better ways.

"Joseph labeled the next tier of Treasures 'profit accelerators.' This makes sense. Treasure 5 (Elevate the Elephants) can significantly improve profit by focusing on the most important priorities while using fewer resources. We have hired an expert 80/20 firm out of Chicago to help us. We are on the way to elevating elephants and accelerating profit. And more profit means more for everyone.

"Genghis Khan showed us in Treasure 6 (Pace The Growth) the power of accelerating growth to achieve long-term goals. He demonstrated the importance of paying attention to time. Any business that can leverage greater sales in less time with similar fixed overheads will profit more. This is another example of realizing more with less. We have reduced our Slinky-effects and have begun to use OKRs (Objectives and Key Results) to keep our pace on track.

"Treasure 7 (A Unique Position: A Better Decision) will increase our sales success. Giotto showed us the importance of perceptions, seeking customer truth, and positioning versus competitive choices. This too will accelerate Peak Precision Parts' profit.

"Regarding the next tier, I've learned that every Treasure shapes our cultural norms to some degree. However, Treasures 8 (Cultivate a Healthy Culture) and 9 (Make Work Simple) are the foundation. Eleanor Roosevelt gave voice to her values. She gave voice to our values. We have codified PPP's values. I particularly like having a 'speed' key-value to reinforce our 3-Keys-Strategy.

"Then there is Alexander Calder. This dream-journey was special. His positive personality was contagious. He personified focusing on simple. Simplifying PPP's work structure and flow by bashing away barriers will make work more enjoyable and help us strive for a Platinum Standard culture.

"That leaves the final dream-journey and tier: Treasure 10 (Intentionally Improve). Joseph calls it the 'sustainability enhancer.' Having Treasure 10 on top makes sense—improvement can apply to everything. I wonder who our sage will be?"

Treasure 9
Make Work Simple

Sage Lesson & Background

Alexander Sandy Calder (1898-1976). Calder symbolizes the need to make work simple and enjoyable by bashing away unhealthy barriers, complexity, and frustration. Calder embraced the principles of simplification and fluidity to create his joyful art.

Calder was an American artist. He is credited as the originator of the mobile. Part of Calder's genius was his ability to connect simple organic forms and colors. He put them into motion through his mechanical sculptures. His work can be found in prominent museums around the world. Calder was awarded The Presidential Medal of Freedom (given posthumously by President Ford in 1977).

Calder's value has increased. In 1941, Solomon Guggenheim paid $233 for a Calder work. On May 13, 2014, Christie's auctioned a Calder hanging mobile titled *Poisson Volant* (Flying Fish), for $25,925,000 USD.

Key Learnings

❑ **Design organizational structure to increase work flow**, foster a healthier culture, and drive competitive advantage. It requires strategic thinking and experimentation to obtain a simple, effective, and enjoyable work flow.

❑ **Bash away barriers**. Remove or minimize obstacles to making work simple. Poor communication, bureaucracy, dysfunction, unnecessary layers, and silos are specific barriers to reduce.

❑ **Streamline communication**. A consistent, simple, unrestricted flow of the right communication is critical to improve work flow. It is essential to maximizing employee effectiveness.

❑ **Reduce silos and reporting layers** but not to the point bottlenecks occur and span of coaching is too wide.

❑ **Eliminate dysfunction** and avoid complicated systems, rules, processes, and procedures that diminish the joy of work and contribute to an unhealthy culture.

❑ Use the **RACI Matrix**, a simple tool that bashes away silo confusion and conflict. RACI clarifies accountabilities, responsibilities, roles, and communications among team members from different silos.

❑ Ensure organizational structure follows strategy. **Connect structure and work flow** to the dream-statement, 3-Keys-Strategy, values, and pace of growth.

❑ The **Ten Treasures are interlinked**. They work together and support each other. When pursued together, enduring success is more likely.

TREASURE

10

INTENTIONALLY IMPROVE

As Elizabeth's grandfather clock strikes twelve, Joseph arrives promptly. She is ready for him. "The question, 'How well does PPP intentionally improve its systems and processes,' scored better than competition. From reviewing the *Ten Treasures Strategic Playbook*, I know Treasure 10 is about intentionally improving to achieve excellence. Who is our sage for our last journey?"

Punxsutawney

"Before answering, here is a question for you: are you familiar with the movie *Groundhog Day*?" She responds, "Yes."

Joseph goes on to talk about the movie and how it relates to Treasure 10 (Intentionally Improve). "Wouldn't it be great to be able to continually improve, the way Phil Connors (Bill Murray) did in the movie? I liked the way the situation was set up—Bill Murray, portraying an egotistical TV weatherman, is forced to go to a small town he hates (Punxsutawney, Pennsylvania). In the monotony of reliving each boring day, Murray learns that life isn't about what happens to you (the dice). He learns it's about purposeful choices as to how to live, and to give. Murray chooses to improve each day to reach a dream—to marry Rita Hanson (Andie MacDowell)."

Joseph continues talking about *Groundhog Day*. "As Murray lives the same day over and over, he grows wiser. He uses the gift of time to improve. He learns to become proficient on the piano, speak fluent French, make beautiful ice sculptures...he memorizes the life stories of the townspeople and helps them."

Joseph states the obvious. "I liked the movie. It prompts the question, if forced to live the same day repeatedly, how would you invest your time?

"We can't redo daily life the way Bill Murray did. But we can choose to improve each and every day. This will help us become more valuable—more indispensable. Our last Treasure will discuss ways Peak Precision Parts can intentionally improve its systems and processes. Doing this every day will help it become more valuable to strategic-customers, employees, you (a shareholder), and society."

Elizabeth asks, "Are we going to Punxsutawney?" Joseph replies, "No. We are going to meet someone who has been an inspiration to you: Marie Curie." Elizabeth smiles.

Paris, Plutonium, and Process Improvement

Elizabeth and Joseph dream-journey to Paris, France. The date is February 2, 1898. They arrive in the 5th arrondissement. The venue is the School of Industrial Physics and Chemistry (now called ESPCI ParisTech). They are in a laboratory with scientific instruments, journals, and natural elements. Marie Curie is focused on taking measurements.

Up until this day, Marie had been working day and night to develop the right processes, tools, and techniques for her scientific experiments. She used thoughtful principles to develop the right methods. There wasn't a ready-made, easy-to-use tool to properly take measurements. Nor was there an established technique. Marie had to make intentional choices to consistently optimize and improve her measurement tools, processes, and techniques. She developed a system that required persistence, dexterity, and concentration. Once optimized, Marie's well-thought-out and innovative system enabled her to take accurate measurements.

Elizabeth and Joseph witness Marie Curie diligently measuring two different chemical elements. She is using an electrometer developed by her husband, Pierre. A chronograph is in her left hand. It calculates the right amount of time needed to take the measurements. Marie is systematically weighing and recording any variations after testing the two elements.

They see Marie carefully write her findings in a gray notebook. She is perplexed. On this day, uranium and thorium produce similar results.

Elizabeth and Joseph travel ahead in time to March 1898. They are still in Marie's laboratory. She is in the same location. It's as though Marie had not left her laboratory. She has thoroughly checked and rechecked her processes to ensure there are no mistakes (eliminate the Gray Zone).

Marie's methodical research reveals a scientific discovery—that another element must be present. She says out loud, that it is "necessary at this point to find a new term to define this new property of matter manifested by the elements of uranium and thorium. I propose the word radioactivity."

After numerous experiments in her laboratory, Marie Curie has discovered that pitchblende is four times more radioactive than uranium or thorium. On July 18, 1898, the Curies announce the discovery of polonium. On December 26, 1898, they announce the discovery of radium.

Marie and Pierre Curie jointly receive the Nobel Prize in Physics in 1903: "In recognition of the extraordinary services they have rendered by their joint researches on the radiation phenomena discovered by Professor Henri Becquerel."

Joseph asks Elizabeth what she has learned from their visits with Marie Curie. Elizabeth responds, "Marie lived her own version of *Groundhog Day*. She had the drive to identify and purposefully fix her errors, repeatedly. She spent considerable time learning, creating, and optimizing until she had the right processes. Excellence and intentional improvement were in her DNA. Without a continuous improvement mindset, she could not have realized her breakthrough discoveries.

"At Peak Precision Parts, I see opportunity to learn from Marie. Even though we scored higher than competition on the Competitive Comparison Question, we must intentionally improve—to ensure our business endures for many generations." Joseph is delighted with her response.

Timeless Improvement Tools

Joseph comments, "We have covered a number of improvement tools throughout our journeys." He hands her a list:

- o Absolute Advantage and 3-Keys-Strategy (Treasure 2).
- o Front-End Thinking (Treasures 2 and 3).
- o Five Steps To Top Talent (Treasure 3).
- o Lean, Value Chain Breakthroughs (Treasure 4).
- o Elevate The Elephants, Eliminate Gray Zones (Treasure 5).
- o The Slinky-Effect, OKRs (Treasure 6).
- o Customer Listening Processes (Treasure 7).
- o The Platinum Standard (Treasure 8).
- o Bash Away Barriers (Treasure 9).

Joseph continues, "There are a handful of additional improvement tools of which you should be aware. They have stood the test of time. They will work today and tomorrow. These include:

o   Process Mapping.
o   Root Cause Analysis.
o   PDCA Improvement Cycle.
o   The Baldridge Performance Excellence Program.
o   Sharper Strategic Planning.
o   Board of Advisors."

Process Mapping

"Let's review each tool starting with process mapping. For successful continual improvement, it is a good idea to get a handle on the existing process. Flow charting (mapping the process) is a good tool to do that.

"Process mapping lets you visually see complexity. It helps you see the activities and steps that make up the process. This helps you identify areas to simplify and improve. What is needed? What can be eliminated? What can be improved or modified? How does it affect the CURVE? Look for improvements that add value. Look to take out steps that diminish value. Look to simplify.

"Process mapping works well with the RACI Matrix (covered in Treasure 9). It should be done by Peak Precision Parts' employees and teams that work the process. Until artificial intelligence and machine learning advances, intentional improvement is a human activity. It is often best when improvement ideas come from employees exposed to the problems and opportunities. They have local knowledge. They are closer to the process. They have more ownership if involved. However, properly train employees before proceeding."

Elizabeth asks, "How do we choose what areas to map?" Joseph responds, "This is a perfect opportunity to elevate the elephants. Process map the most important. Start with your 3-Keys-Strategy. Specifically, the strategic-customer purchase process is worth mapping.

"Other areas to map include strategic areas within the value chain. These could include how Peak Precision Parts assembles rapid prototype materials. Consider customer delivery and product return processes—anywhere that is strategic in the value chain—especially areas that improve speed and accuracy. Process mapping can help you visualize where to pursue value chain breakthroughs.

"Besides value chain activities, you can map the most important areas in Treasures 3, 8, and 9. Mapping areas such as these can improve the health of the organization.

"An area to look for improvements are hand offs—physical and communication handoffs. These transitions are error prone. They often need improvement. Another area to look for improvements are work-arounds (make-shift solutions that have not been given proper attention).

"Clear and accurate process maps will make it easier for employees to discover where improvements can be made to the process."

Root Cause Analysis

Joseph discusses the next timeless tool. "Intentional improvement seems straight forward. It is, if you go about it the correct way. For maximum effectiveness, it requires accurate problem and opportunity definition. You want to uncover the root cause of problems that lead to the right improvement opportunities.

"If you do not uncover the root cause of problems, they will likely persist. Many organizations have a whack-a-bat mentality. They see a problem and immediately 'whack it' to quickly fix it.

"For simple problems, this may be okay. For more complex problems, it is worth investing time upfront to analyze what is truly causing the problem (front-end the thinking). Go deeper than identifying a symptom. You want to peel back the onion and identify the root cause of the problem.

"After the root (problem or opportunity) is identified, it's time to create an action plan. This is followed by measuring to ensure improvement is occurring as planned. When delving into complex process or product (service) failures, it is wise to use standard, proven methods for documenting and getting to the core. There are a wide range of approaches, tools, and techniques to uncover the root cause.

"Train employees in root cause analysis tools and techniques. This will go a long way to ensure you are solving the right problems correctly. If leadership and the culture embrace it, everybody should at least be familiar with basic root cause analysis skills, regardless of job title or position in the company.

"Customers value problem solvers. Having a company armed with the right problem-solving tools and techniques can lead to a competitive advantage. The American Society for Quality has good materials and training to learn the right root cause analysis tools and techniques."

Joseph refers to Marie Curie. "Curie's approach to identifying polonium and radium were based on a form of root cause analysis."

PDCA Improvement Cycle

Next, Joseph introduces Plan Do Check Act (PDCA). He hands her a PDCA diagram from the Playbook. "One of the early pioneers of quality, W. Edwards Deming, created a tool called the PDCA Improvement Cycle. It applies to any improvement opportunity or situation that requires change. This simple tool breaks improvements into four steps. As you can see, the four steps are visualized in a circle. They are repeated (hence, the word cycle). That means the steps are continually evaluated and updated. PDCA reminds me of Bill Murray in *Groundhog Day*. Murray lived in an improvement loop. He chipped away each and every day until he achieved excellence."

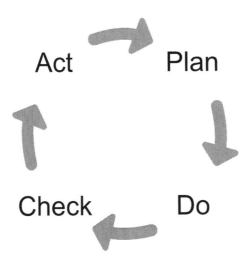

Act   Plan

Check   Do

Joseph provides an overview of each of the four PDCA steps:

o **PLAN** "Typically, you start by thinking about the obstacles and opportunities. Gather relevant data. Conduct *root cause analysis* to identify the problems or opportunities to improve. Plan your outcomes, including setting objectives and key measures."
o **DO** "Take action by putting into place the activities required for improvement. Make the improvements."

- CHECK "Check, evaluate, and review the improvement results. Use facts. Measure your success relative to your starting point."
- ACT "Document the improvements. Identify further improvement opportunities. Adjust or tweak improvements, as learning dictates. Incorporate improvements into the operating procedures of the organization. Repeat the PDCA process."

Baldridge Performance Excellence Program

Joseph provides Elizabeth with information on The Baldrige Performance Excellence Program. "This is a United States public-private partnership dedicated to performance excellence.

"The Baldrige Program raises awareness about the importance of performance excellence. It provides useful and free organizational assessment tools and criteria. Baldridge educates leaders about the practices of best-in-class organizations. It recognizes and honors national role models with the Presidential Award for performance excellence.

"I am a former Baldridge Examiner. In this role, I evaluated and provided feedback to organizations across the United States. Baldrige is a good framework to improve Peak Precision Parts' performance. It is designed to drive sustainable results. It applies to many organizations. A systems approach to improve your organization's performance is provided by the Baldrige framework."

Joseph hands Elizabeth a diagram of the Baldrige framework:

He continues, "It consists of categories (criteria). They are integrated and linked. The criteria begin with Leadership and conclude with Results. Objective measurement, analysis, and knowledge management are used in all categories. The underlying basis of the Baldrige criteria is a set of values and concepts. These are embedded beliefs and behaviors found in high-performing organizations. We covered these in several of the Treasures, especially Treasure 8 (Cultivate A Healthy Culture)."

Sharper Strategic Planning

Joseph reminds Elizabeth that strategic planning is an important intentional improvement tool. She comments, "I am familiar with SWOT (Strengths, Weaknesses, Opportunities, Threats) analysis and other strategic planning approaches from my days at the hospital. Answering the right questions you have posed to me throughout our journeys will provide PPP with a more useful and valuable strategic plan. Are there additional points or steps to consider for our strategic plan?"

Joseph replies, "To answer your question, this will be a long answer. Let's start with a few points. Solving the right problems leads to more success. Strategic planning is about solving the right problems in the right order as the world changes.

"In your business, only a handful of things do not change. Your values are timeless. Your dream-statement remains constant unless it is realized (this rarely occurs). Your 3-Keys-Strategy evolves. However, it is not changed on a whim. Other than those few items, everything else will change over time. Peak Precision Parts will need to adjust and refine its choices.

"Speaking of adjustments, that reminds me of an important lesson learned as a boy. While on vacation, my grandfather, Woodhull Powell, taught me how to sail. He was a former sea captain out of Gloucester. On a perfect, end of summer day, I asked him to take me sailing one last time before our family returned to the Midwest.

"Woodhull said, *'Let's check the glass.'* He went over to his trustworthy barometer and tapped it. With a concerned look, he turned to me and said, *'Sorry Swabby, bad weather's approaching.'* Later that day, a Nor'easter came through. He taught me the importance of leading indicators and the need to adjust plans.

"Back to strategic planning. It is not a straight-line improvement process. The status quo will not last. You will confront 'bad weather' in the form of gravity-shifts. It's important to have accurate business barometers—leading indicators so that you can gain the advantage of adjusting early.

"There are many was to plan. Find a method and process that works for you and that fits your culture. How deep and involved you want to go is up to you. Regardless, there are five action steps that good strategic plans should consider following. The first three involve more thinking than doing. The last two involve more doing than thinking."

Joseph shares his Five Strategic Planning Action Steps overview illustration from the Strategic Playbook:

Five Strategic Planning Action Steps

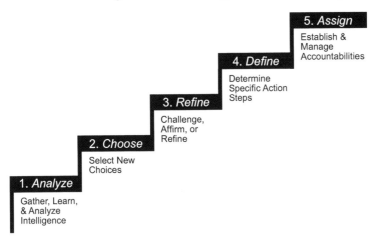

Joseph continues, "Here is a detailed outline of each step." Joseph hands Elizabeth a document from the Playbook. Elizabeth reads it carefully.

1. *Analyze*—**Gather, Learn, & Analyze Intelligence**
   a. Analyze what's next. Start with an assessment of gravity-shifts (positive and negative trends) that can affect Peak Precision Parts. For example, overseas price competition or a growing need for complex, mission-critical medical devices.
   b. Gather intelligence from Peak Precision Parts' customers, employees, suppliers, competitors, and important stakeholders. Collecting this information is ongoing. Pay particular attention to objective external customer feedback (relative to competition). You already have your internal Competitive Comparison Questions

survey results. Update results for each strategic plan revision (rank order and index results, low to high). Analyze the feedback.

c. Analyze your competitive advantages, as perceived by current and prospective strategic customers. Identify areas along the value chain that you can build on and strengthen. Find and innovate value chain breakthroughs. Identify the most important ways to improve your value chain, 3-Keys-Strategy, and CURVE (Customer Unique and Relative Value Equation).

d. Analyze your competitive disadvantages. These are strategic customer requirements where you are underperforming along the value chain versus other choices (based on a hierarchy of needs). Fix the strategic value chain disadvantages which are most important to strategic customers. Look to turn these into sustainable advantages.

e. Analyze major bottlenecks. Learn what is the most important thing that is holding you back from achieving your long-term (TRUE) goal, and pursuing your dream-statement.

f. Analyze what your best leading indicators are telling you. If PPP does not use leading indicators, identify and understand the most objective leading indicators for your industry and the economy. You need to know the time gap between the indicator and the change. Using good business barometers will enable PPP to proactively pivot and adjust sooner.

g. Ask then analyze what you don't know. This is best asked of others that do know.

   i. An advisory or board of directors is a good place to ask what you do not know but should.

   ii. Peer learning organizations are another way to learn what you don't know (NAWBO-National Association of

Women Business Owners, YPO-Young
Presidents Organization, Vistage, EO-
Entrepreneurs' Organization...).
  iii. TED, industry, leadership, innovation,
       and other conferences are good places to
       learn what you don't but ought to know.
  h. Analyze how you did. Assess how well PPP
     performed on its most recent strategic plan
     review or deep dive. Analyze why there were
     errors. Apply learnings to improve.

2. *Choose*—Select New Choices
  a. Choose the most important improvements to
     make (in priority order).
  b. Choose the most important new opportunities
     identified in the Ten Treasures that can help
     (dream-statement, pace the growth, five steps to
     top talent, elevating the elephants, cultivate a
     healthy culture, and the like).
  c. Choose what you are *not going to do*. Often
     times, strategic plans add a ton of new activity.
     The "to do" list expands. It's important to create
     a "take away" list of less important activities.
     Elevating the elephants will help with this task.
     Identify No Zone items and say no to them.
     Eliminate the most important Gray Zones.

3. *Refine*—Challenge, Affirm, or Refine Existing Choices
  a. Refine the existing choices. Challenge the
     organization to eliminate, continue, or improve
     existing choices.
  b. Refine, build on, and better leverage PPP's
     competitive advantages along the value chain.
     Discover *value chain breakthroughs*—new
     activities that solve old problems in entirely new
     and better ways.
  c. Reduce disadvantages (based on 1.c, and 1.d
     findings) along the value chain.

d. Refine STAR talent and succession plans.
e. Refine PPP's priorities. Focus on the elephants. Challenge and get rid of low priorities that do not contribute to achieving PPP's TRUE goal and improving the CURVE. Eliminate activities that are in conflict with PPP's values and future strategic direction.
f. Improve pace of growth and agility.
g. Bash away barriers and simplify organizational structure to make work easy to do.
h. Refine processes.
i. Work towards an ideal culture: The Platinum Standard. Prioritize opportunities to cultivate a healthy culture.

4. *Define* — Determine Specific Action Steps
a. Define the most important objectives, goals, strategies, and tactics.
  i. Ensure that the right (most important) measures are in place for the strategic dashboard.
b. Engage all managers and employees to define specific action steps linked to the strategic plan.
  i. Break down the TRUE and other long-term strategic plan goals into shorter term action steps.
  ii. Align specific action steps among employees, as appropriate.

5. *Assign* — Establish & Manage Accountabilities
a. Have each person develop strategic plan OKRs.
  i. Avoid redundancy by sharing and reviewing all OKRs.
  ii. Follow up on strategic plan OKRs.
b. Assign performance review accountabilities (who does what and by when).
  i. Follow up on the performance review accountabilities, as appropriate.

Execution

Joseph continues thoroughly answering the question about Peak Precision Parts' strategic plan. "Up to this point, the Ten Treasures cover the first three action steps reasonably well. The last two action steps (4. *Define* and 5. *Assign*) need discussion."

Joseph makes his next point with emphasis. *"Having the right follow-through on strategic plans is equal in importance to making the right strategic choices."*

"You want to ensure that the long-term strategies and objectives are translated into shorter time periods. Break down the TRUE and other long-term strategic plan goals into yearly and quarterly objectives and measurable key outcomes (OKRs).

"Pursue activities that are the best option you can pursue within the shorter defined time periods with current available resources and constraints to move the strategic plan forward. Identifying shorter term, doable steps focusses managers on practical, measurable outcomes. It helps the organization move the plan forward one quarter and one year at a time.

"Align these shorter term objectives and measurable key outcomes among all employees at Peak Precision Parts. Ensure each employee *owns* a piece of the strategic plan with specific accountabilities. Incorporate accountabilities into Peak Precision Parts' performance management system."

Elizabeth asks if he can say more about accountabilities. Joseph does so. "After you engage your team in answering the broader strategic questions and determine specific action steps, determine who owns the responsibility. More specifically, *who* is going to do *what* and by *when*.

"Peak Precision Parts' strategic plan is not complete until every division, functional area, department, and employee has mid-term and short-term accountabilities that flow from the broader, long-term plan. These accountabilities give the plan traction. They are essential to long-term success."

Frequency

Elizabeth asks, "What is the right frequency to reevaluate or revise our plan?" Joseph replies, "Effective strategic planning is a journey; not an event. A good strategic plan is continually improved. It is not a static document that sleeps in file.

"Conduct frequent and ongoing strategy conversations with the leadership team. Focus on the most important strategic issues. Formally review the plan each year.

"If meaningful new intelligence is uncovered from leading indicators, customers, or there are significant gravity-shifts before the annual review, that is the time to reevaluate and improve the plan. Do a deep dive every three to five years or sooner, if there is meaningful learning, growth, or material declines."

Joseph hands Elizabeth a Playbook diagram that depicts the Five Strategic Planning Action Steps as an intentional and ongoing improvement process, revolving around PPP's 3-Keys-Strategy, dream-statement, TRUE goal, and values:

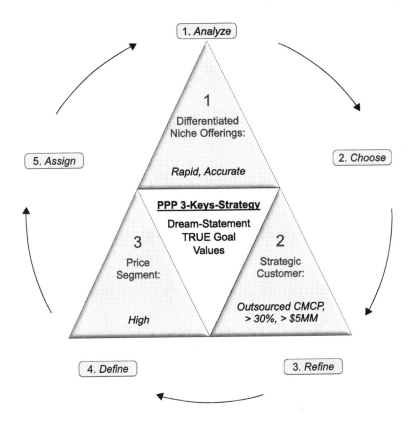

Board of Advisors

While on the topic of strategic planning and improvement, Joseph asks why she hasn't considered a board of advisors. Elizabeth says she has but recently joined a peer-learning organization forum and the National Association of Women Business Owners. Joseph encourages her to do more. "These are excellent opportunities to learn. Consider a board of advisors in addition to remaining in your peer-learning organizations. A board complements these. There are three material differences with an advisory board:

1. You pick the expertise. The board should have the right experts to help solve PPP's most important problems and realize the most important opportunities identified in the strategic plan. Key items from the strategic plan

are typically on the agenda in most advisory or fiduciary board meetings.
2. You set the agenda. The members are deeply and fully devoted to Peak Precision Parts (time is not shared with other businesses).
3. You can selectively evolve the board's expertise based on changing strategic needs."

Joseph continues, "A board populated with experts who possess the right wisdom will help Peak Precision Parts get to the next levels. They will challenge you on important strategic and policy topics. They will help you intentionally improve. However, a good board takes time to lead and run properly. It is one of those investments that the more you put in, the more you get out.

"You now have a timeless and comprehensive toolkit to intentionally improve."

No Drinking From A Firehose Rule

Elizabeth thanks Joseph and asks, "Do you have any final thoughts on integrating all these useful ideas into Peak Precision Parts?"

"Yes. Establish the *No Drinking From A Firehose Rule* and stick to it. To increase the odds of success and avoid becoming overwhelmed, before the leadership team (or any team in the organization) takes on a new project, it must first remove a lower priority project. This will minimize the drinking from a firehouse effect that often occurs when new wisdom comes onstream. More importantly, it will activate leadership."

Twice Nobel

"Before we say goodbye, let's make a final journey."

Elizabeth and Joseph dream-journey to an assembly hall in Stockholm, Sweden. The date is December 10, 1911. There is a large, well-dressed crowd of distinguished people. Elizabeth and Joseph hear an announcement by Dr. E. W. Dahlgren. He is the President of the Royal Swedish Academy of Sciences:

> "This year, the Academy has decided to award you the prize for *Chemistry* in recognition of the eminent services you have rendered to this science…
>
> "This is the first time that the distinction has been conferred on a previous prizewinner. I beg you, Madame, to see in this circumstance a proof of the importance which our Academy attaches to your most recent discoveries, and I invite you, Madame, to receive the prize from His Majesty the King, who has graciously consented to present it to you."

Elizabeth and Joseph listen to Marie's Nobel Prize acceptance speech. She pays tribute to her husband Pierre but makes it clear that her work was independent from his. Marie details their separate contributions and describes the discoveries she has made after Pierre's death.

After her speech, Elizabeth congratulates Marie. She asks her a question. "Do you have any advice for me? I admire you and what you have accomplished. I am looking to make a difference in the world, too."

Marie responds, "You cannot hope to build a better world without improving the individuals. To that end, each of us must work for his own improvement and, at the same time, share a general responsibility for all humanity, our particular duty being to aid those to whom we think we can be most useful."

Treasure 10
Intentionally Improve

Sage Lesson & Background

Marie Sklodowska Curie (1867-1934). Curie serves as a role model to leverage intentional improvement (mindset and tools) every day throughout the organization to sustain success. Intentionally improving systems and processes increase an organization's value to society, improves competitive advantage, and enhances all of the Treasures.

Marie Curie was a Polish scientist (chemist and physicist). She was the first woman to receive a PhD degree from a French university, become a faculty member at the École Normale Supérieure (1900), and win the Nobel Prize (Physics, 1903). Marie Curie was the first *person* to win the Nobel Prize a second time (Chemistry, 1911) and only person to win in two different sciences.

Marie was a multifaceted woman of intensity, intelligence, and determination. Her commitment to improvement enhanced her value to society.

Key Learnings

❏ Make intentional improvement part of your company and its culture. Be mindful to **improve each and every day**.

❏ **Leverage timeless improvement tools**. Process mapping identifies where improvements should be made. Root cause analysis identifies core problems and opportunities. The PDCA Cycle breaks the improvement process into four repeatable steps (Plan, Do, Check, Act). The Baldrige Performance Excellence Program provides useful leadership and organizational assessment tools and criteria.

❑ Strategic planning is an important method of improvement. It involves solving the right problems in the right order as the world changes. It's about making the **right choices of what to do and what not to do**.

❑ The **Five Strategic Planning Action Steps** are worth considering. They apply to many strategic planning processes.

❑ Having the **right follow through** (execution) on strategic plans is equal in importance to making the right strategic choices. Translate the TRUE (Tied to Profit; Risk-aligned; Unmistakable; Explosive) goal and important next steps into shorter term objectives and measurable key outcomes. Align and share these with every employee. **Establish and manage accountabilities**—who is going to do what and by when.

❑ Effective strategic planning is a journey, not an event. Conduct **frequent and ongoing strategy conversations** with the leadership team and board (if you have one).

❑ Review the plan each year. Do a deep dive every three to five years. **Make adjustments** to the plan sooner, if there is meaningful learning, growth, or material declines.

❑ A **board of advisors** (or directors) is a good place to ask what you do not know but should. They will challenge you on important strategic issues. They will help you intentionally improve and achieve enduring success.

EPILOGUE

TRUE TREASURE

It's late on Sunday evening. Elizabeth is reminiscing about the ten dream-journeys. She can't believe how fortunate she is to have learned so much from Joseph and the sages. It has been a life changing adventure.

Her grandfather clock rings one bell. Joseph won't be coming to take her on another dream-journey. The baton has passed to her. She has the responsibility to lead and share the Ten Treasures with all Peak Precision Parts' managers and employees. She is off to a good start. However, there are many miles to travel on her true journey.

She picks up the *Ten Treasures Strategic Playbook* and reviews it. She notices something that wasn't there before. It's a handwritten note. She recognizes the writing:

You always had the thirst to learn, the drive, and the leadership skills to turn around PPP...now you have the wisdom.

The truest treasure you can give to yourself and the world is to use your newly found insight to turn Peak Precision Parts into a unique, enduring, and extraordinary company — one that adds value to and changes our world for the better.

Joseph

BIBLIOGRAPHY

o   1968 National NCAA Men's Basketball Final Recap –
     UCLA vs. UNC. 1968. Retrieved on December 21, 2016
     from www.youtube.com/watch?v=t_k9LBuRriU
o   1968 National NCAA Men's Basketball Semifinal Game –
     UCLA vs. Houston. 1968. *The Game of The Century.*
     Retrieved on December 21, 2016 from
     www.youtube.com/watch?v=uAOCWXm1TfQ
o   Abdul-Jabbar, Kareem. 2017. *Coach Wooden and Me: Our
     50-Year Friendship on and Off the Court.* Grand Central
     Publishing.
o   Baal-Teshuva, Jacob. 1999. *Calder.* Taschen.
o   Beaulieu, Brian, and Beaulieu, Alan. *Prosperity In The Age
     Of Decline.* 2014. John Wiley & Sons.
o   Birkinshaw, Julian and Heywood, Suzanne. 2010. Putting
     Organizational Complexity In Its Place, McKinsey &
     Company, May 2010.
o   Butman, John. 1997. *Juran: A Lifetime of Influence.* Wiley
o   Calder, Alexander. 1977. *Calder: An Autobiography with
     Pictures.* Pantheon; First THUS Edition.
o   Center For Disease Control and Prevention. 2018. *Average
     Life Expectancy.* Retrieved on May 30, 2018 from
     www.cdc.gov/nchs/fastats/life-expectancy.htm
o   Collins, Jim. 2001. *Good To Great. Why Some Companies
     Make The Leap…and Others Don't.* Harper Business.
o   Collins, Jim., and Porras, Jerry. 1994. *Built to Last:
     Successful Habits of Visionary Companies.* HarperBusiness.
o   Cope, Tim. 2015. *On the Trail of Genghis Khan: An Epic
     Journey Through the Land of Nomads.* Bloomsbury USA.
o   Cotter, John. J. 1995. The 20% Solution: Using Rapid
     Redesign to Create Tomorrow's Organizations Today.
     Wiley.
o   Curie, Eve., and Sheean, Vincent (translator). 2001. *Madame
     Curie: A Biography.* Da Cap Press; Reissue Edition.
o   Daly, Mark. 2005. *5 Steps To Board Success! New
     Approaches to Board Effectiveness and Business Success.*
     AuthorHouse.
o   Davis, Johnny. 2011. "10 Years of The iPod." *The
     Guardian*, March 18, 2011. Retrieved on May 21, 2017 from

www.theguardian.com/technology/2011/mar/18/death-ipod-apple-music

o Defeo, Joseph. A., and Juran, Joseph. M. 2010. *Juran's Quality Handbook: The Complete Guide to Performance Excellence 6/e*. McGraw-Hill Education.

o Doerr, John. 2018. *Measure What Matters: How Google, Bono, and the Gates Foundation Rock the World with OKRs*. Portfolio/Penguin.

o Drucker, Peter. F. 2008. *The Essential Drucker: The Best of Sixty Years of Peter Drucker's Essential Writings on Management*. Collins Business Essentials.

o Dunnell, Ruth. W. 2009. *Chinggis Khan (Library of World Series)*. Pearson.

o Easterbrook, Gregg. "What Happens When We Live To 100?" *Atlantic*, October 2014.

o Edwards, Benj. "The iPod: How Apple's Legendary Portable Music Player Came To Be." *Macworld*, October 23, 2011. Retrieved on December 28, 2016 from www.macworld.com/article/1163181/consumer-electronics/the-birth-of-the-ipod.html

o Ericsson Global Key Figures Mobility Report: Smartphone 2023 Forecast. Retrieved on May 30, 2018 from www.ericsson.com/en/mobility-report/reports/november-2017/key-figures

o Flores d'Arcais. Francesca. 2012. *Giotto*. Abbeville Press.

o Ford, Henry. 1988. *Today and Tomorrow – Special Edition of Ford's 1926 Classic*. Productivity Press.

o Ford, Henry., Crowther, Samuel. 1922. *My Life and Work*. Doubleday Page & Company.

o Friedman, David. J. 2018. *Culture by Design, 8 Simple Steps to Drive Better Individual and Organizational Performance*. High Performing Culture, LLC.

o Gerber, Robin. 2002. *Leadership the Eleanor Roosevelt Way: Timeless Strategies from the First Lady of Courage*. Prentice Hall.

o Godin, Seth. 2011. *Linchpin: Are You Indispensable?* Portfolio.

o Godratt, Eliyahu. M., and Cox, Jeff. 1984. *The Goal: A Process of Ongoing Improvement*. North River Press.

o Goldsmith, Barbara. 2005. *Obsessive Genius: The Inner World of Marie Curie*. W. W. Norton.

o Harnish, Verne. 2014. *Scaling Up: How a Few Companies Make It and Why the Rest Don't*. Gazelles, Inc.

- Heath, Chip., and Heath, Dan. 2007. *Made To Stick: Why Some Ideas Survive and Others Die*. Random House.
- Hirt, Martin. *Don't Omit This Crucial Detail From Your Strategic Roadmap: The First Step*. McKinsey & Company Strategy & Corporate Finance Blog. December 13, 2018. Retrieved on December 18, 2018 from www.mckinsey.com/business-functions/strategy-and-corporate-finance/our-insights/the-strategy-and-corporate-finance-blog
- Holiday, Ryan. *Lessons On Power and Leadership From Genghis Khan*. Forbes. May 7, 2012. Retrieved on December 17, 2018 from www.forbes.com/sites/ryanholiday/2012/05/07/9-lessons-on-leadership-from-genghis-khan-yes-genghis-khan/#18fb2e4b6996
- Isaacson, Walter. 2011. *Steve Jobs*. Simon & Schuster.
- Jobs, Steve. 2001. *Steve Jobs Introduces Original iPod – Apple Special Event (2001)*. YouTube. Retrieved on December 28, 2016 from www.youtube.com/watch?v=SYMTy6fchiQ
- Juran, Joseph. M. 2003. *Architect of Quality: The Autobiography of Dr. Joseph M Juran*. McGraw Hill.
- Keller, Scott., and Meaney, Mary. *Attracting and Retaining The Right Talent. McKinsey & Company*, November 2017.
- Khan, Paul. 2005. *Secret History of the Mongols: The Origin of Chingis Khan*. Cheng & Tsui.
- King, Martin Luther. Jr. 1963. "I Have A Dream…" (original speech manuscript). *National Archives*. Retrieved on May 29, 2018 from www.archives.gov/files/press/exhibits/dream-speech.pdf.
- King, Martin Luther. Jr. 1968. "I've Been To The Mountaintop" (speech). *The Martin Luther King, Jr. Research and Education Institute. Stanford University*. Retrieved on May 29, 2018 from www.kinginstitute.standford.edu/encyclopedia/ive-been-mountaintop
- Koch, Richard. 1999. *The 80/20 Principle: The Secret to Achieving More with Less*. Currency.
- Koch, Richard. 2013. *The 80/20 Manager: The Secret to Working Less and Achieving More*. Little, Brown and Company.
- Lacey, Robert. 1986. *Ford: The Men and the Machine*. Little Brown & company.

o   Lean Enterprise Institute. *What Is Lean?* Retrieved on December 15, 2018 from www.lean.org/WhatsLean/

o   Lencioni, Patrick. 2002. *The Five Dysfunctions Of A Team.* Jossey-Bass.

o   Liker, Jeffrey. K. 2004. *The Toyota Way: 14 Management Principles from the World's Greatest Manufacturer.* McGraw-Hill.

o   Lopreato, Joseph. 1965. *Vilfredo Pareto.* Thomas Y. Crowell Company.

o   Magretta, Joan. 2011. *Understanding Michael Porter: The Essential Guide to Competition and Strategy.* Harvard Business Review Press.

o   Marter, Joan. M. 1992. *Alexander Calder (Cambridge Monographs on American Artists).* Cambridge University Press.

o   Museum Of Modern Art. 1943. *Museum Of Modern Art Opens Exhibition of Calder Mobiles...*original press release. Retrieved on December 28, 2016 from www.moma.org/documents/moma_press-release_325413.pdf

o   Pareto, Vilfredo. 1971. *Manual of Political Economy.* Augustus M Kelley Publishers (New English Translation).

o   Perry, Mark. J. AEI.org. October 20, 2017. *Fortune 500 firms 1955 c. 2017: Only 60 remain thanks to creative destruction that fuels economic prosperity.* Retrieved on May 30, 2018 from www.aei.org/publication/fortune-500-firms-1955-v-2017-only-12-remain-thanks-to-the-creative-destruction-that-fuels-economic-prosperity/

o   Porter, Michael. E. 1980. *Competitive Strategy.* The Free Press.

o   Porter, Michael. E. 1998. *Competitive Advantage: Creating and Sustaining Superior Performance.* The Free Press.

o   Rath, Tom. 2007. *Strength-Finders 2.0.* Gallup Press.

o   Ries, Al., and Trout, Jack. 2000. *Positioning: The Battle for Your Mind.* McGraw-Hill.

o   Roosevelt, Eleanor. 2014. *The Autobiography of Eleanor Roosevelt.* Harper Perennial: Reprint Edition.

o   Rubin, Danny., and Ramis, Harold. 1993. *Groundhog Day* (film). Directed by Harold Ramis. Studio: Columbia Pictures.

- Segall, Ken. 2012. *Insanely Simple: The Obsession That Drives Apple's Success*. Portfolio / Penguin.
- Schlender, Brent., and Tetzeti, Rick. 2016. Becoming Steve Jobs: *The Evolution of a Reckless Upstart into a Visionary Leader*. Crown Business.
- Snow, Richard. 2014. *I Invented the Modern Age: The Rise of Henry Ford*. Scribner Reprint Edition.
- Sweeney, James Johnson. 1943. *Alexander Calder*. The Museum of Modern Art. Original exhibition catalogue. Retrieved on December 21, 2016 from www.moma.org/calendar/exhibitions/2870
- Tate Museum Exhibition. Liverpool, England. June 6 – October 5, 2014. *Mondrian And His Studios*. Retrieved on December 28, 2016 from www.tate.org.uk/whats-on/tate-liverpool/exhibition/mondrian-and-his-studios
- The American Experience (PBS Film). Director and Writer: Williams, Sue. Producer: Dietz, Kathryn. Narrator: McCullough, David. 2000. *American Experience Eleanor Roosevelt*. Full transcript retrieved on May 29, 2018 from www.pbs.org/whph/americanexperience/films/eleanor/
- The Arbinger Institute. 2000. *Leadership and Self Deception: Getting Out of the Box*. Berrett-Koehler.
- Weatherford, Jack. 2004. *Genghis Khan and the Making of the Modern World*. Three Rivers Press (Crown Publishing Group).
- Wikipedia. 2018. *Giotto*. Retrieved on May 29, 2018 from en.wikipedia.org/wiki/Giotto.
- Wolf, Norbert. 2006. *Giotto (Taschen Basic Art)*. Taschen.
- Woloch, Nancy, PhD. 2017. Eleanor Roosevelt's White House Press Conferences, September 22, 2017. Retrieved on November 20, 2018 from NWHM (National Women's History Museum). https://www.womenshistory.org/articles/eleanor-roosevelts-white-house-press-conferences
- Woloch, Nancy, PhD. 2017. *Eleonor Roosevelt In Her Words: On Women, Politics, Leadership, and Lessons from Life*. Black Dog & Leventhal.
- Wolper, David. L. 1963. *Biography: Eleanor Roosevelt*. Twenty-six-minute film directed by Alan Landsburg. Hosted and Narrated by Mike Wallace. Retrieved on May 29, 2018 from www.youtube.com/watch?v=msUrOD6B9ul
- Womack, James P. 2003. *Lean Thinking: Banish Waste and Create Wealth in Your Corporation*. Free Press.

o   Wooden, John. 1997. *Wooden: A Lifetime of Observations and Reflections On and Off the Court*. Contemporary Books.
o   Wooden, John. 2009. *Coach Wooden's Pyramid of Success*. Revell.

IMAGE CREDITS

All images, illustrations, and designs by Mark Daly, except the following:

Cover Concept: Art Direction: Jeff Walker, Design: Ian O'Saben, VSA Partners, Inc.

Payne Map of the World: The World from the Best Authorities map by John Payne, 1798. Photographic reproduction of public domain image from Wikimedia Commons (Wikimedia.org). Image cropped and converted to black and white.

Ford Magneto Assembly Line Workers: Ford Highland Park Michigan assembly line photo taken circa 1913. Public domain image from Wikimedia Commons (Wikipedia.org).

1943D Penny: Coin sold by Legend Numismatics, Lincroft, New Jersey for $1.7 million. Image from Coinupdate website, September 23, 2010. (coinupdate.com). Image modified (removed background and imperfections, converted to black and white).

Roosevelt Press Conference: Photo taken March 6, 1933 by Harris & Ewing, Inc. Image from Library of Congress, Franklin D. Roosevelt Presidential Library Museum (fdrlibrary.com).

Morning Star: Image created in Affinity Designer by the author based on images from *Alexander Calder* by Joan M. Marter (page 208, Cambridge University Press), and the MoMA (Museum of Modern Art) website. Alexander Calder, 1943. Gift of the Artist. MoMA object number 848.1966. © 2019 Calder Foundation, New York / Artists Rights Society (ARS), New York.

Baldridge Diagram: Image created in Affinity Designer by the author based on an image from the Baldridge Performance Excellence Program, 2018-2019. Baldridge Excellence Framework: A Systems Approach to Improving Your Organizations Performance. Gaithersburg, MD. U.S. Department of Commerce, National Institutes of Standards and Technology.

Author Photograph: Photo taken in Lisbon, Portugal by Gigi Daly.

INDEX

10K documents, 111
1600 Pennsylvania Avenue, 171
1943D copper Lincoln penny, 161
20/20 foresight, 56
3-D printing, 44
3-Keys-Strategy, vi, xii, 56, 57,
    58, 59, 60, 61, 62, 64, 67, 75,
    85, 97, 100, 103, 108, 112,
    117, 126, 128, 129, 130, 131,
    138, 148, 150, 165, 167, 170,
    187, 195, 211, 215, 216, 219,
    223, 225, 230, 232, 236
5 Steps to Board Success, viii
80/20, 122, 123, 125, 138, 139,
    141
A Social Media Dream, 29
Absolute advantage, vi, 56, 67,
    109, 215, 223
Accountability, 42, 135, 150, 152,
    193, 205, 206, 207, 208
Acura, 115
Adoration of the Magi, 157
Affordable Care Act, 43
Aileron, 179
Alcohol drinkers, 123
Alexander Calder, xi, 196, 197,
    213, 216
Alexander The Great, 147
Align, 30, 39
Align the organization, 26
Altai Mountains, 144
Amazon, 109, 151
American Red Cross, 172
American Society for Quality,
    106, 226
Andie MacDowell, 220
Andy Grove, 151
Apple, 46, 47, 48, 49, 50, 51, 52,
    53, 54, 55, 56, 58, 66, 187
Arena Chapel, 157, 159, 169
Arno, 156
Artificial Intelligence, 43
Average Lifespan, 43
Baghdad, 146
Baldrige, 199, 228
Bash Away Barriers, 203, 218,
    223, 234

Basket-of-givens, 5, 8
Bauhaus, 47
Beijing, 146
Benjamin Franklin, 70
BHAG, 32
Big Hairy Audacious Goal, 32
Bill Murray, 220, 221, 227
Bing, 43
Bishop Charles Mason Temple, 22
Board of Advisors, 224, 237
Boardwalk and Park Place, 3, 4
Bureaucracy, 204, 205, 206, 211,
    212, 218
Business-to-Business, 163, 164
Calculated risks, 100
Calder, 196, 197, 198, 199, 200,
    201, 202, 203, 204, 207, 212,
    213, 218
Cargill, 179
CD players, 49
Cellphones, 46
Centric cultures, 177, 194
Chaos theory, 125
Chicago, 95, 216
Chief Nursing Officer, 2
Christie's, 218
Civil rights activist, 41
CliftonStrengths, 63
Coach Wooden, 70, 71, 72, 76, 80,
    84, 92, 121, 182, 215
Comcast, 179
Common sense, 8
Competitive advantage, xi, xii, 5,
    13, 14, 15, 17, 19, 25, 27, 29,
    39, 45, 54, 56, 61, 64, 66, 67,
    73, 81, 84, 96, 99, 100, 106,
    108, 109, 110, 113, 116, 117,
    124, 133, 141, 145, 146, 151,
    154, 167, 176, 187, 191, 211,
    215, 218, 226, 240
Competitive Comparison
    Questions, 9, 13, 17, 24, 63,
    73, 118, 231
Competitive disadvantage, 14, 232
Confusing signs, 28
Congressional Gold Medal, 41
Constitution Hall, 175

Consultants, xiii, 3, 8, 32, 183
Continuous improvement, xii, 223
Conway Family Business Center
    survey, 180
Cuisinart, 47
Cultivate a Healthy Culture, ix,
    20, 196, 216
Cultural compatibility, 76
Cultural foundation, 20, 216
Cupertino, 48, 52, 53
CURVE, vi, xii, 12, 13, 14, 15, 16,
    17, 19, 32, 37, 45, 57, 58, 61,
    65, 82, 83, 89, 98, 108, 112,
    113, 114, 116, 117, 123, 191,
    211, 215, 224, 232, 234
Customer relationship
    management, 164
Customer touchpoints, 159, 164,
    170
Customer Unique and Relative
    Value Equation, 13, 14, 32, 45,
    98, 123, 215, 232
Customer-Centric, 178
Data analytics, 164
Daughters of American
    Revolution, 175
Define The Dream, x, 19, 41, 114,
    214
Define Your Price Segment, 57
Denver Mint, 162
Design talent, 47
Differentiated niche offerings, 57,
    59, 67, 97, 107, 127, 131, 187
Disney, 55
DNA, viii, 46, 76, 207, 223
Dr. E. W. Dahlgren, 239
Dr. Martin Luther King Jr., 21, 24,
    26, 41, 214
Dream-statement, xii, 25, 26, 27,
    29, 30, 31, 36, 38, 39, 40, 41,
    42, 46, 53, 59, 64, 75, 85, 96,
    99, 100, 103, 131, 133, 145,
    150, 152, 153, 154, 177, 181,
    184, 192, 198, 211, 214, 215,
    219, 230, 232, 233, 236
Drucker, 153
DuckDuckGo, 43
Dysfunction, 37, 177, 204, 206,
    210, 212, 218, 219
Easy to Share, 27, 30, 40
EBITDA, 33
École Normale Supérieure, 240

Eleanor Roosevelt, xi, 171, 173,
    174, 175, 180, 181, 182, 185,
    194, 216
Elephant's rule, 120, 141
Elevate The Elephants, 19, 120,
    122, 124, 126, 139, 141, 148,
    191, 210, 223, 225
Elizabeth Schulte, xiii
Elvin Hayes, 68
Emancipation Proclamation, 21
Employee Promise, 188, 189
Enrico degli Scrovegni, 158
Entrepreneurs, xiii
ESPCI ParisTech, 221
ESPN, 92
Everybody's business, 136
Excellence, xi, 7, 9, 220
Explosive, 32, 35, 42, 128, 154,
    215, 241
Facebook, 30
Family businesses, xiii, 179
Family-Centric, 178, 179
FATE guidelines, 23, 26, 29, 38,
    39, 41, 214
FDR, 173
Feast of the Annunciation, 158
Fernand Leger, 197
FireWire, 50
Five score years ago, 22
Five Steps to Successful
    Succession, vi, 84, 93
Five Steps To Top Talent, vi, 73,
    92, 223, 233
Five Strategic Planning Action
    Steps, 231, 236
Fixed assets, 110
Flow charting, 224
Flywheel magneto, 94, 95
Focus groups, 164
Force for good, 32, 42
Ford, 44, 95, 96, 97, 98, 99, 100,
    101, 102, 103, 112, 113, 114,
    116, 121, 179, 218, 250
Fortune 500, 43, 179, 259
Fragmented culture, 176
Frederick the Great, 130
Free cash flow, 38
Front-end the thinking, 49, 54, 74,
    103, 223, 226
Front-line employees, 108, 117,
    206
Future Dream, 26, 30, 39

Gap list, 88, 89
Garbage in garbage out, 183
GDP, 123, 179
General Motors, 114
Genghis Khan, xi, 143, 144, 146, 147, 216
George W. Bush, 92
Georgia Institute of Technology, 125
Gettysburg Address, 22
Giotto, xi, 156, 157, 158, 159, 160, 162, 163, 166, 167, 169, 216
Giving-Centric, 178, 180
Glassdoor, 77
Gloucester, 230
GM, 44, 114
Good customers, 126, 128
Good in good out, 183
Good strategy, 15, 46
Google, 43, 151
Gravity-shifts, vi, xii, 43, 44, 46, 47, 54, 55, 64, 66, 100, 114, 115, 133, 148, 155, 162, 164, 178, 230, 231, 236
Gray Zone, 137, 138, 139, 140, 142
Great Depression, 114
Greater potential to make a difference, 20
Greatest Generation, 200
Groundhog Day, 220, 221, 223, 227
Halley's Comet, 158
Hayes, 72
Henry Ford, xi, 95, 96, 99, 101, 102, 104, 109, 113, 116, 215
Henry McBride, 200
Hewlett Packard, 55
Hierarchy of needs, 102, 116, 232
Highland Park, 96, 99, 100, 101, 250
HMO's, 43
Houston Astrodome, 68
Houston Cougars, 68, 69
I Have a Dream, 23, 41, 121
Inclusion-Centric, 178
Indiana, 10, 73, 156
Indianapolis, 2, 9, 10
Infiniti, 115
Innovation, x, 44, 46, 47, 48, 49, 53, 62, 123, 215, 233

Innovation Leader, 63, 65, 76, 85, 86, 89
Innovation-Centric, 178
Innovative work process, 95
Insights, x, xi, 5, 7, 53, 65, 103, 160
Instagram, 30
Intel, 151
Intentional Improvement, 20, 217, 220, 240
Interview panel, 80
Intuitively obvious, 48
iPod, 47, 49, 51, 52, 53, 55, 61, 167
ISO 13485, 28
iTunes, 50
James Ferris, 48
James Johnson Sweeney, 199
Jamugha, 144, 146
Jane Powell, 11, 12
Japanese, 44, 114
Jazz, 44
Jean Arp, 197
Jerry Porras, 32
Jesus Christ, 158
Jim Collins, 32
Jim Womack, 104
Joan Magretta, 113
Joan Miro, 197
Jobs, 21, 46, 47, 48, 49, 51, 52, 53, 54, 55, 56, 66
John Doerr, 151
John Wooden, xi, 69, 76, 92
Jon Rubinstein, 50
Joseph Ford, 125
Joseph Juran, 119
Joseph Powell, xiii, 3
Juran, 119, 122
Kareem Abdul-Jabbar, 68, 76
Kennedy, 30
Key-value, 187, 216
Khan, 144, 145, 146, 147, 154
King, 21, 22, 23, 41, 121
Koch Industries, 179
Lausanne, Switzerland, 118
Lean, xii, 103, 104, 105, 106, 115, 117, 223
Leonardo da Vinci, 203
Levi's, 48, 52
Lew Alcindor, 68, 76
Lexus, 115
Lightbulb question, 81, 82

Lincoln, 21, 161, 162, 174, 175
Lincoln Memorial, 21, 174, 175
LinkedIn, 77
Lorraine Motel, 23
Lynn Shackelford, 72
Macintosh, 48
Macworld, 50
Magnetic pull, 77
Mahalia Jackson, 22
Major League Baseball, 122
Make Work Simple, xi, 20, 212, 216, 218
March on Washington for Jobs and Freedom, 21
Marian Anderson, 174
Marie Curie, xi, 213, 221, 222, 223, 226, 239, 240
Mark Daly, iv, viii, 250, 259
Mars, 179
Master spotter, vi, 46
McDonald's, 77, 78
McKinsey, 122
Measure What Matters, 152
Medieval, 157, 159, 167
Memphis, 22, 23
Michael Porter, 45, 106, 113
Michelangelo, 157
Michigan, 250
Millennials, 180
Mind, Money, and Muscle, 2
Mini, 61
MIT's International Motor Vehicle Program, 104
Mobile ethnography research, 103, 164
Model T, 44, 94, 95, 96, 97, 98, 99, 101, 103, 109, 113, 114
Modernism, 44
MOMA, 199, 200, 202
Mongolia, 143
Monopoly, 3, 4, 7, 15, 125, 161
More remarkable, better future, 25, 41
Morning Star, 201
MP3, 50
My Day, 174
Nano, 61
National Association of Women Business Owners, 2, 233, 237
NCAA basketball, 68
NCAA Coach of the Century, 92
NCAA Men's Semi-Finals, 72

Net profit, 33
Net Promoter Score, 102
New York, Tennessee, and Saint James Place, 3
News Corp, 179
Niche The New, ix, x, 19, 44, 45, 46, 47, 51, 53, 55, 62, 65, 66, 67, 76, 85, 114, 126, 148, 162, 167, 215
No Drinking From a Firehose Rule, 238
No Zone, 137, 139, 140, 142, 233
Noah, 119
Nobel Peace Prize, 41
Nobel Prize in Physics, 223
No-Customers, 128
Non-profit, xiii, 19, 180
No-products, 131, 132
Off-the-grid, 44
OKRs, xii, 151, 152, 153, 155, 212, 216, 234, 235
Operational Discipline, xi, 19, 106, 116
Organizations isolate culture from strategy, 20
Overhead creep, 111
Ownership-Centric, 178
P-68, 51, 52, 53
Pace the growth, 105, 145, 146, 147, 148, 150, 154, 191, 206, 219, 233
Padua, Italy, 157, 158, 169
Pareto, 119, 122, 123, 141
Paris, France, 196, 221
Patrick Lencioni, 206, 211
Paul McCartney, 38
Pauley Pavilion, 69
PDCA Improvement Cycle, 224, 227
Peer-learning organization, xiii
Perception equals reality, 160
Performance Metrics, 75
Persia, 146
Peter Drucker, 153
Peter Philippi, viii
Pew Research Center, 122
Phil Connors, 220
Phil Shiller, 51
Philanthropy, xii
Piet Mondrian, 196, 197, 198
Platinum Standard, 192, 195, 216, 223, 234

Poisson Volant, 218
Poor communication, 204, 212
Poor Vision, 27
Pop art, 44
Pope, 157
Porsche, 47, 48
Portable music players, 47, 51
Porter, 113
Position versus competitive
    choices, 167
President Ford, 218
Presidential Medal of Freedom,
    41, 92, 218
Process Mapping, 224
Professionals, xiii
Professor Henri Becquerel, 223
Profit accelerators, 19, 136, 216
Punxsutawney, Pennsylvania, 220
Purpose statements, 25
Pyramid of Success, 69
Quality improvement disciplines,
    106
RACI, 208, 209, 210, 219, 224
Red Petals, 202
Reduce waste, 15, 32, 104, 117,
    141
Reference checking, 82
Renaissance, 157, 169
Representational realism, 44
Research objectives, 103
Responsible, Accountable,
    Consulted, Informed, 208
Return on invested capital
    (ROIC), 33
Return on invested human capital
    (ROIHC), 33
Reverse engineer, 111, 176
Right Talent Definition, 74, 92
Risk Factor, 33
Risk tolerance, 34, 35, 40, 42
Risk Tolerance Continuum, 34
Rita Hanson, 220
Ritz-Carlton, 188, 189, 190, 191
Rock-and-roll, 44, 162
ROI, 112, 113, 134, 135, 142
Rolling Stones, 55
Roman Empire, 147
Root Cause Analysis, 224, 225
Roxbury, Connecticut, 202
Royal Swedish Academy of
    Sciences, 239
S1 documents, 111

San Francisco, 50
School of Industrial Physics and
    Chemistry, 221
Screening tools, 79, 134
Scroll-wheel, 51, 53
Secret History of the Mongols,
    145
Seek the truth, 163
Service value chain, 108
Sharper Strategic Planning, 224,
    229
Shuffle, 61
Silos, 207
Simplification and fluidity, 203,
    218
Sistine Chapel, 157
Six Sigma, 106
Slinky-effect, 149, 150
Smartphones, 51
Social media, 29, 30, 31, 164, 165
Solomon Guggenheim, 218
Sony Walkman, 49
Sony's Discman, 49
Star of Bethlehem, 157, 158, 162
Stars, 82, 83, 87, 93, 134, 215
Star-Spangled Banner, 175
State Highway Patrol, 10
Steve Jobs, x, 46, 48, 51, 53, 54,
    56, 63, 66, 121, 215
Stewardship, xii, 192
Stock Keeping Units, 91, 131
Stockholm, Sweden, 239
Story of five blind individuals,
    160
Strategex, viii
Strategic compass, 24, 25, 26, 214
Strategic customers, 57, 58, 59,
    75, 102, 111, 112, 126, 127,
    128, 130, 132, 134, 162, 163,
    165, 211, 232
Strategic Dashboard, 36, 37, 42
Strategic foundation, 19, 41, 214
Strategic plan, 9, 229, 232, 233,
    234, 235
Strength-Finders, 63
Success Characteristics, 63, 65, 76
Succession plan, 1, 84, 87, 89, 93,
    215, 234
Sustainability enhancer, 20, 217
Sustainability-Centric, 178
SWOT analysis, 229

Tap The Top Talent, xi, 19, 92, 101, 134, 183, 188, 215
Targeted marketing, 77
Teach Strategy, 27, 30, 39
Teaching Treasures, 5, 6, 8
TEAMS guidelines, vii, xii, 181, 195
Technology disruptions, 46
Technology-Centric, 178
TED, 233
The Baldridge Performance Excellence Program, 224, 228
The Game of the Century, 68
The Pareto Principle, 119, 122
The Platinum Standard, 192
The real battleground, vii, 160, 166
The Right Questions, 6, 8, 112, 126, 140, 177, 211, 229
Tied To Profit, 32
Toshiba, 50
Touch, 61
Toyota, 103, 104
Transfer knowledge, 7
Transformative change, xiii, 26, 39
Transformative journey, 24
Treasure 1, x, 19, 41, 114, 214
Treasure 10, xi, 20, 217, 220, 240
Treasure 2, x, 19, 66, 76, 85, 114, 115, 126, 162, 215, 223
Treasure 3, xi, 19, 92, 101, 183, 188, 215, 223
Treasure 4, xi, 19, 116, 215, 223
Treasure 5, xi, 19, 141, 216, 223
Treasure 6, xi, 19, 143, 154, 216, 223
Treasure 7, xi, 20, 168, 169, 216, 223
Treasure 8, xi, 20, 194, 196, 223, 229
Treasure 9, xi, 20, 196, 214, 223, 224
TRUE goal, vi, xii, 31, 32, 33, 35, 36, 37, 40, 42, 85, 88, 89, 145, 152, 153, 211, 215, 234, 236

Turnover, 74, 83, 101, 123
Tuscan, 156
Twitter, 30, 151
UCLA Bruins, 68, 72
Unique Position, xi, 19, 169, 216
Uniquely position, 157, 159, 165, 169
Uniquely positioned, 159, 166
United States, iv, 41, 96, 116, 166, 174, 175, 228
Unmistakable, 32, 35, 42, 128, 154, 215, 241
Unprofitable race to the bottom, 29
Value chain, xii, 96, 100, 106, 107, 108, 109, 110, 112, 113, 117, 135, 165, 215, 225, 232, 233
Value Chain Breakthroughs, vi, 106, 112, 223, 225, 232, 233
Venice, 157
Vilfredo Pareto, xi, 119, 121
Virgin Mary, 158
Vistage, 233
VOC, 102, 103
Voice of the Customer, 102, 164
Volkswagen Beetle, 48
W. Edwards Deming, 227
Walmart, 179
Washington D.C., 174
Washington Mall, 21, 175
We shall overcome someday, 21
What gets measured gets done, 32
WIIFM, 78
Wikipedia, 43
Win more and lose less, 5, 166
Winning-Centric, 178
Wooden, 69, 70, 71, 72, 76, 84, 92
Work trial period, 79
Yes Zone, 137, 139, 140, 142
Yes, No, & Gray Zones, vi, 136, 222
YouTube, 30
YPO, 3, 233
Zappos, 188

ACKNOWLEDMENTS

Ten Treasures Strategic Playbook would not be the best version of itself without important contributions from others.

My greatest gratitude goes to Gigi Daly, my best friend, cheerleader, and wife for life. She has been there from the start. Her instincts have been spot on. She has provided excellent insight, editorial suggestions, and support. Thank you for sticking to your opinions, even when I was not so happy to hear them, and caring enough to hang in there and make the book great. This publication and my world would not be complete without you.

I am very grateful to Gregg Daly, my son and in-house family editor. He reviewed every page on so many occasions that I can't remember how many. The book is significantly better off from his rigorous, generous, highly responsive help and from his exceptional command of the written word. There is no one better.

I received *many* in-depth suggestions from a handful of people who were most generous with their time. The book is much better in its content, readability, usability, and relevance from the tremendous help of Peter Philippi (who also wrote the foreword), Alan Abrams, Kevin Bright, Steve Cobb, Lisa Jennings, Lisa Pruett, Rob Reifsnyder, Joanne Spigner, Steve Steinman, and Jim Wilz. I can't thank you enough!

Valuable ideas, feedback, and guidance were also provided by Jim Akers, Steven Daly, Dave Dillon, CW Mundy, Rebecca Mundy, Cindy Petrie, Wym Portman, Arthur Powell, Gordy Rich, Walter Solomon, and Al Stuempel. Thank you for improving the book.

Thanks go out to my son and brilliant technology expert, Patrick Daly. He patiently taught me how to use vector graphics software to create the book's images and illustrations.

Special thanks to Jim Hallene, Jeff Walker, and Ian O'Saben from VSA Partners. They are true professionals in the design world and developed an impactful cover concept—consistent with the "brand" of Ten Treasures.

The two main characters honor my parents (Joseph and Elizabeth Daly) and Gigi's parents (Arthur and Jane Powell).

Learning is a two-way street. I want to acknowledge the business people and advisors who helped with the research and validation phases of the book and who taught me as we worked together to create exceptional, enduring organizations. By the way, Peak Precision Parts (PPP) is fictional. Any resemblance to an actual company is coincidental.

ABOUT THE AUTHOR

Mark Daly imagines a world where every business has extraordinary and enduring success. Quality of life is enhanced from better goods and services. Workers learn, grow, and prosper. Customers and communities are enriched. There is more for everyone. Mark believes his dream can come true—one leadership team and company at a time.

Mark has forty years of business experience and 125 years of board service in a variety of industries from the Inc. 500 to the Fortune 500 (dalystrategic.com). He wrote *5 Steps To Board Success! New Approaches to Board Effectiveness and Business Success*, a book for mid-sized company boards. Mark is a graduate of Cornell University and Wharton (MBA).

In addition to business wisdom, Mark has been blessed with several God-given talents. As an American impressionist painter, he has won major national art awards, is represented by prominent galleries, and is collected worldwide (markdaly.com). Mark plays the mandolin, composes original music, and is on a variety of recordings, including two solo albums. He is a Voting Member of the Grammys (mandomusic.com). These experiences help him to think and strategize in unique and creative ways so that businesses and people can achieve the success they want.

35159158R00151

Made in the USA
Lexington, KY
01 April 2019